THE BLUEGRASS SONGBOOK • PIANO/VOCAL/GUITAR

ISBN 978-1-4584-1649-0

HAL•LEONARD® CORPORATION

7777 W. BLUEMOUND RD. P.O. BOX 13819 MILWAUKEE, WI 53213

ANGEL BAND

Words and Music by
RALPH STANLEY

Moderate Country

My lat - est sun _____ is _____
Oh, bear my long - in' _____

sink - in' fast. My race is near - ly
heart _____ to Him who bled and died _____ for

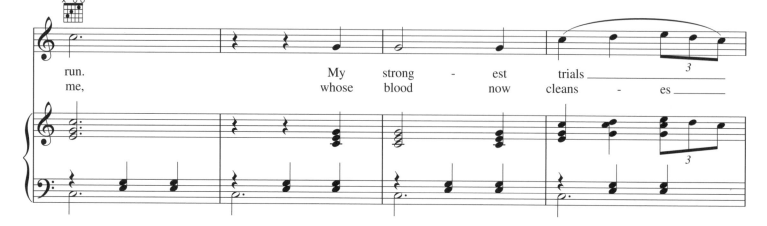

run.
me, My strong - est trials _____
whose blood now cleans - es _____

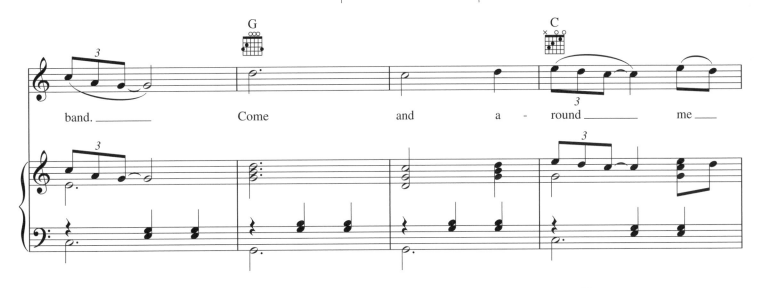

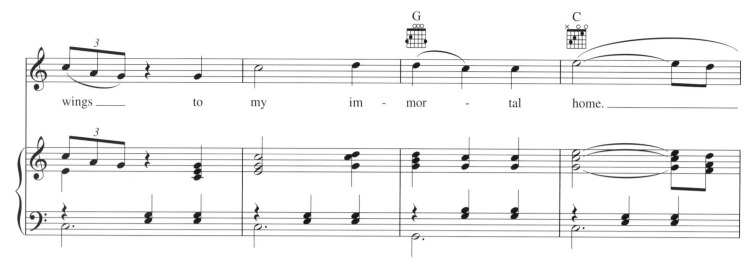

wings _____ to my im - mor - tal home. _____

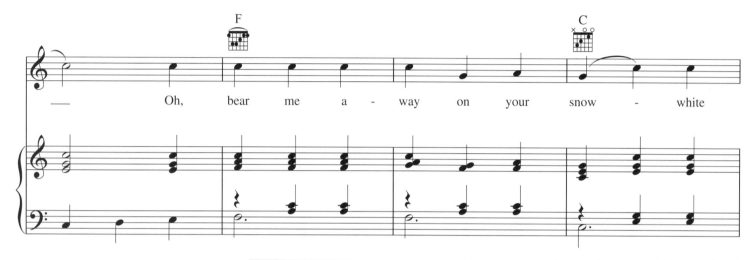

Oh, bear me a - way on your snow - white

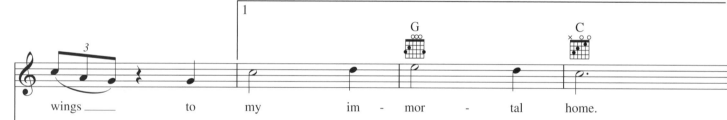

wings _____ to my im - mor - tal home.

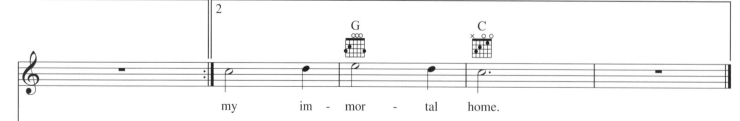

my im - mor - tal home.

rit.

BIG SPIKE HAMMER

Words and Music by BOBBY OSBORNE
and PETE GOBLE

Can't you

hear   the   rhy - thm   of   my   big   spike   ham - mer?
best   ham - mer   swing - er   in   this   big   sec - tion   gang.
been   lots   of   plac - es,   not   much   I   ain't   done.

Lord,   it's   bust - in'   my   side.   I've   done
Big   Bill   John - son   is   my   name.   This   black
Still   some   things   I'd   like   to   see.   But   this

all I can do to keep that ___ wom-an,
ham - mer I swing for a dol-lar and a half a day, ___
ham - mer I swing or the wom - an ___ that I love, ___

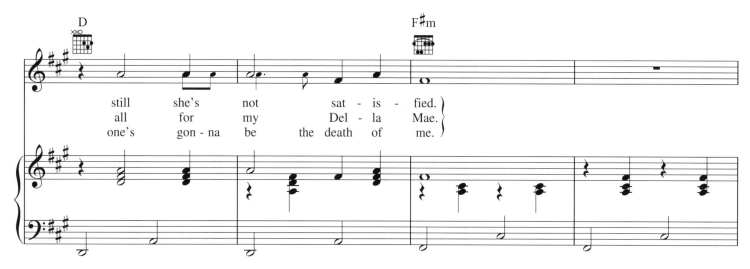

still she's not sat - is - fied.
all for my Del - la Mae.
one's gon - na be the death of me.

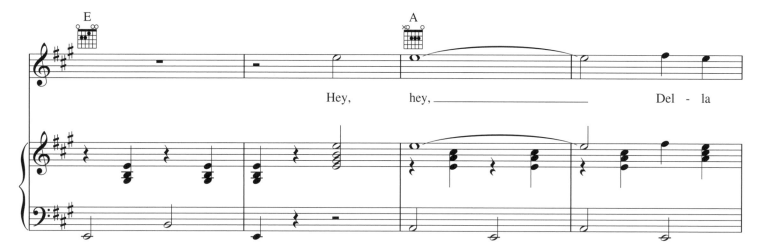

Hey, hey, ___ Del - la

Mae, why do you treat me this ___

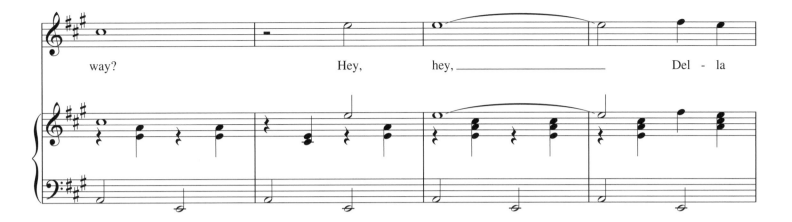

way?   Hey, hey, _____   Del - la

Mae,   I'll get e - ven some __ day.

F#m E A

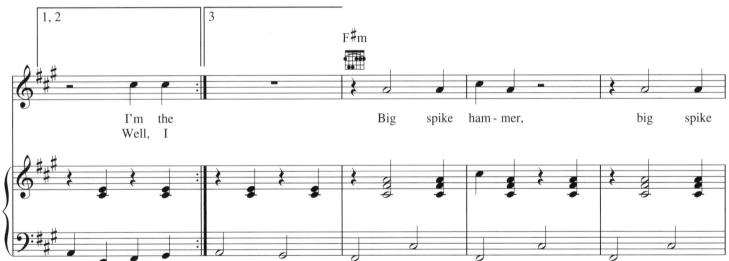

1, 2   3   F#m

I'm the   Big spike ham - mer,   big spike
Well, I

E   A   E A

ham - mer.

BALLAD OF JED CLAMPETT

from the Television Series THE BEVERLY HILLBILLIES

Words and Music by
PAUL HENNING

Come and lis-ten to my sto-ry 'bout a man named Jed,
first thing you know old Jed's a mil-lion-aire,
Jed bought a man-sion, law-dy, it was swank,
now it's time to say good-bye to Jed and all his kin.

poor moun-tain-eer, bare-ly kept his fam-'ly fed. And
kin-folk said, "Jed, move a-way from there." Said,
next-door neigh-bor was the pres-'dent of the bank. Lot-sa
They would like to thank you folks for kind-ly drop-pin' in. You're

then one day, he was shoot - in' at some food, and
"Cal - i - for - ny is the place you ought - a be." So they
folks ob - ject - ed, but the bank - er found no fault, 'cause
all in - vit - ed back a - gain to this lo - cal - i - ty to

up through the ground came a - bub - bl - in' crude.
load - ed up the truck and they moved to Bev - er - ly.
old Jed's mil - lions was a - lay - in' in the vault.
have a heap - in' help - in' of their hos - pi - tal - i - ty.

Oil, that is!   *Black gold,*   *Texas Tea!*
Hills, that is!   *Swimmin' pools,*   *movie stars!*
Cash, that is!   *Capital gains,*   *depletion money!*
Hillbilly, that is!   *Set a spell,*   *take your shoes off!*

Well, the   *Y'all come back, ya hear?*
Old
Well,

BAREFOOT NELLIE

Words and Music by JIM DAVIS
and DON RENO

1. Bare-head-ed wood-peck-er sit-tin' on a limb,
2. Pig-let hog walk-in' in the knot,
3. Nel-lie went to town one day,
4., 5. *See additional lyrics*

ma said chick-en, but Nel-lie got him. Wrung his neck and
make three tracks in just one knot, Nel-lie says, "Who do you
rid-in' on a load of hay. Sold a man a

picked him clean, the fun-ni-est chick-en I've ev-er seen.
think I am?" That hog's miss-in' a-bout one ham.
trip to Mars and now she sits be-hind the bars.

Hey, bare - foot Nel - lie, oh, bare -

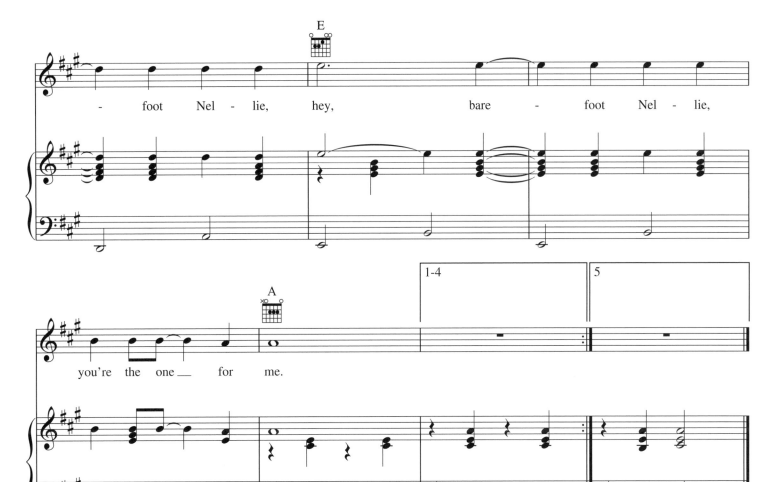

- foot Nel - lie, hey, bare - foot Nel - lie,

1-4   5

you're the one __ for me.

Additional Lyrics

4. Nellie put on her Sunday dress, thought that it would look the best.
   Made out of an old feed sack, hog feet growed right on the back.

5. Nellie's got a pair of shoes, she can wear 'em if she choose,
   So why the heck she got the blues? Who wants to wear size twenty-two?

BLUE MOON OF KENTUCKY

Words and Music by
BILL MONROE

moon keep __ on a - shin - in' bright __ you're gon - na bring-a me back - a my

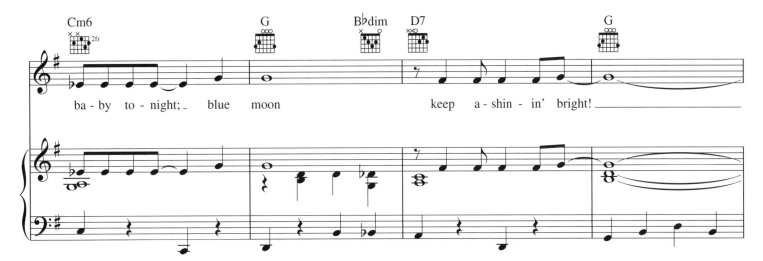

ba - by to - night; __ blue moon keep a-shin - in' bright! _____

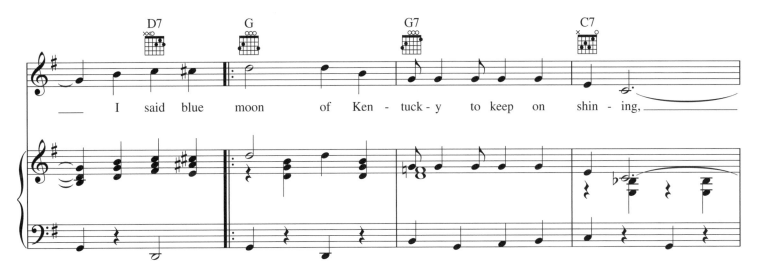

__ I said blue moon of Ken - tuck-y to keep on shin - ing, _____

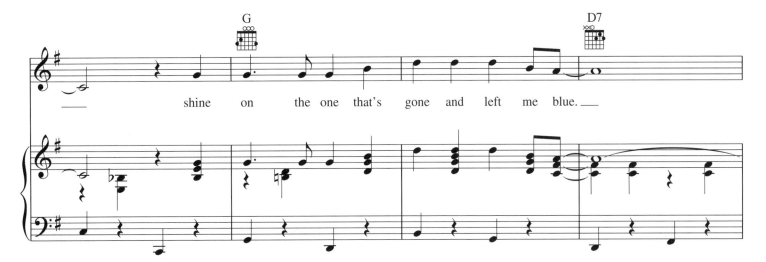

__ shine on the one that's gone and left me blue. __

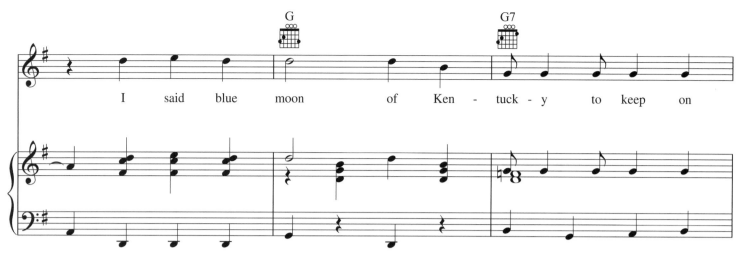

I said blue moon of Ken - tuck - y to keep on

shin - ing, _____ shine on the one that's

gone and left ___ me blue. ___ Well, it was

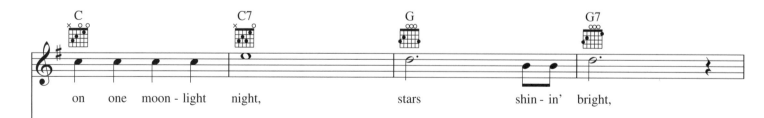

on one moon - light night, stars shin - in' bright,

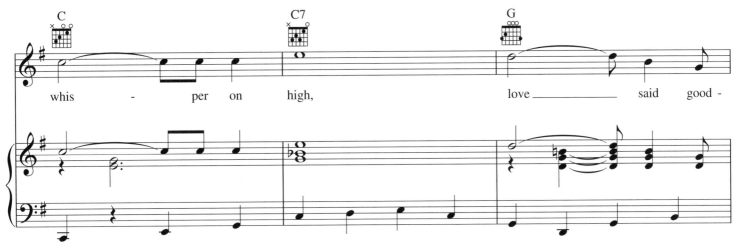

whis - per on high, love _____ said good -

bye. Blue moon of Ken - tuck - y, keep on shin - ing, _____

shine on the one that's gone and left ___ me blue. _

I said blue _____

BLUE RIDGE CABIN HOME

Words and Music by LOUISE CERTAIN
and GLADYS STACEY

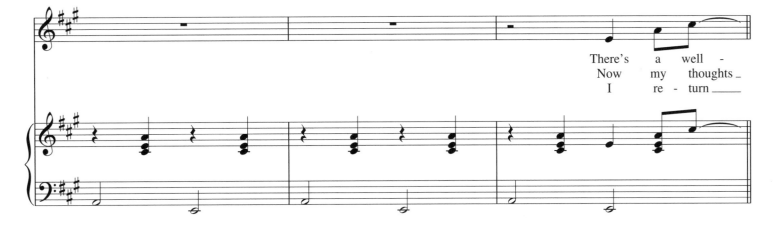

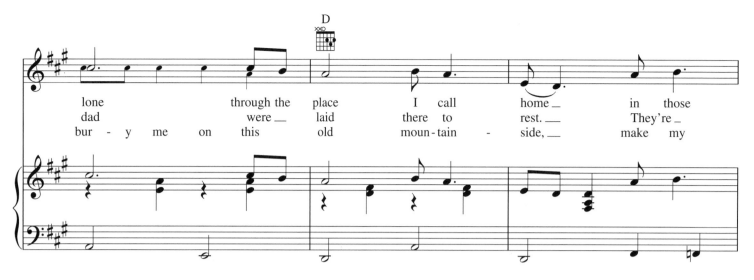

lone through the place I call home __ in those
dad were __ laid there to rest. __ They're __
bur - y me on this old moun - tain - side, __ make my

Blue Ridge hills __ far a - way. __
sleep - ing in peace __ to - geth - er there.
rest - in' place on the hills so high. __

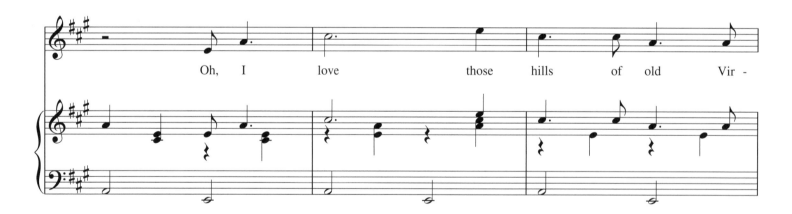

Oh, I love those hills of old Vir -

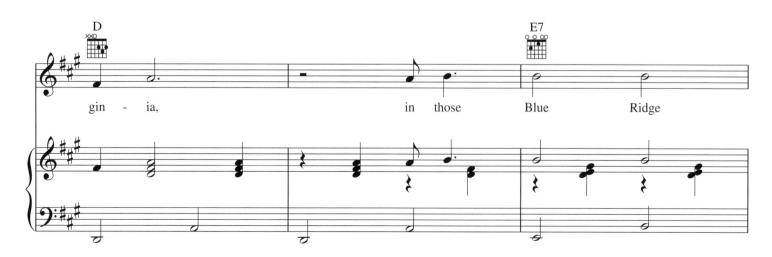

gin - ia, in those Blue Ridge

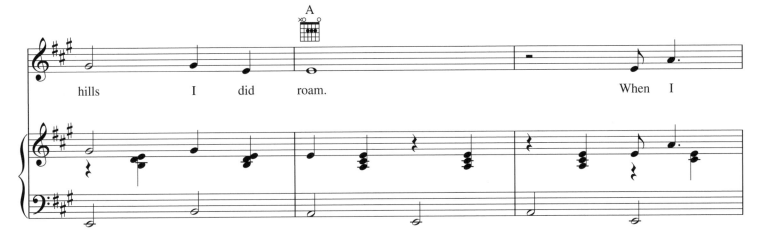

hills I did roam. When I

die, won't you bur - y me on the moun - tain

far a - way near my Blue Ridge Moun - tain

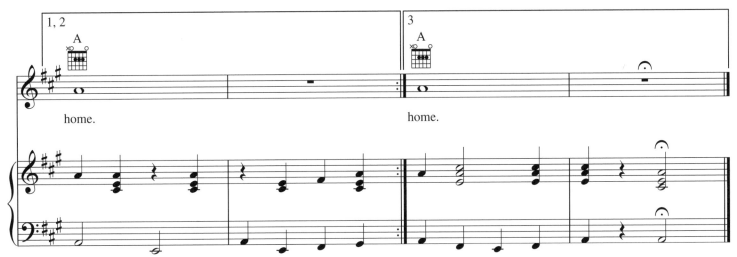

1, 2

home.

3

home.

BLUE TRAIN

Words and Music by
DAVE ALLEN

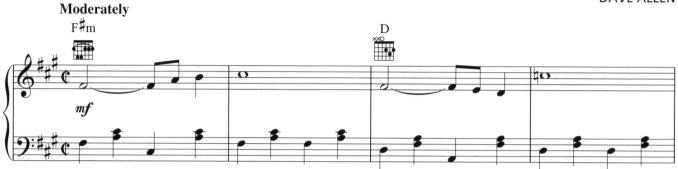

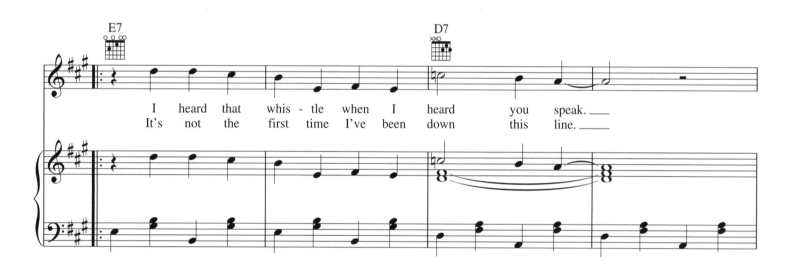

I heard that whis-tle when I heard you speak. ___
It's not the first time I've been down this line. ___

Felt that rum-ble un-der-neath my feet. ___
I've done some trav-'lin' with this heart of mine. ___

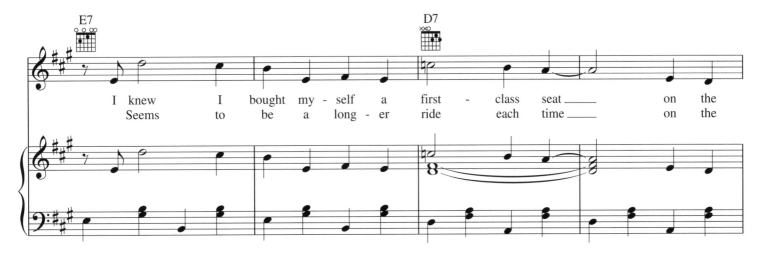

I knew I bought my-self a first - class seat ___ on the
Seems to be a long-er ride each time ___ on the

blue train. ___
blue train. ___

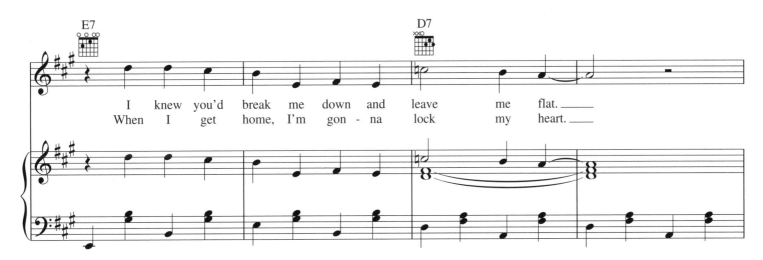

I knew you'd break me down and leave me flat. ___
When I get home, I'm gon-na lock my heart. ___

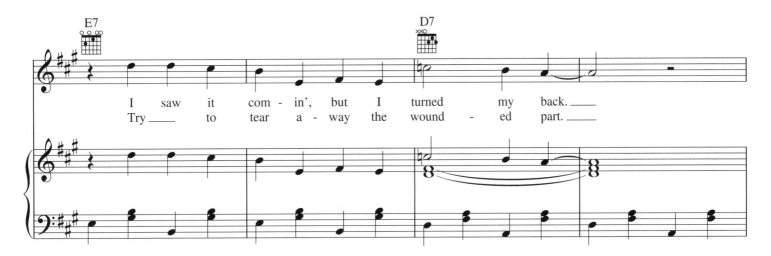

I saw it com - in', but I turned my back. ___
Try ___ to tear a - way the wound - ed part. ___

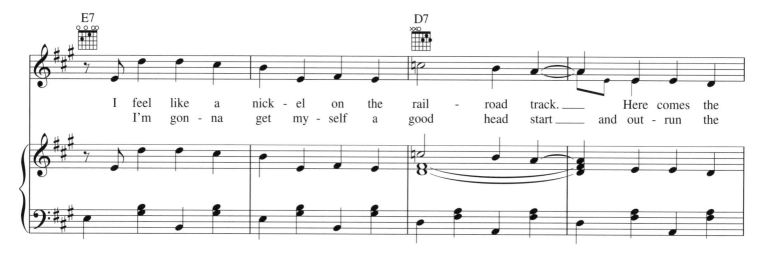

I feel like a nick-el on the rail-road track.____ Here comes the
I'm gon-na get my-self a good head start ____ and out-run the

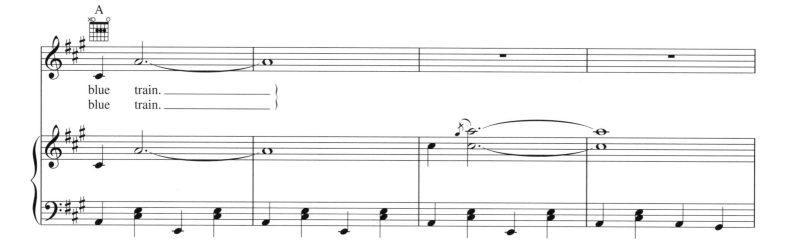

blue train. _____
blue train. _____

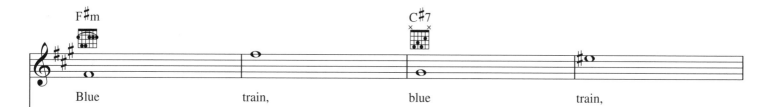

Blue train, blue train,

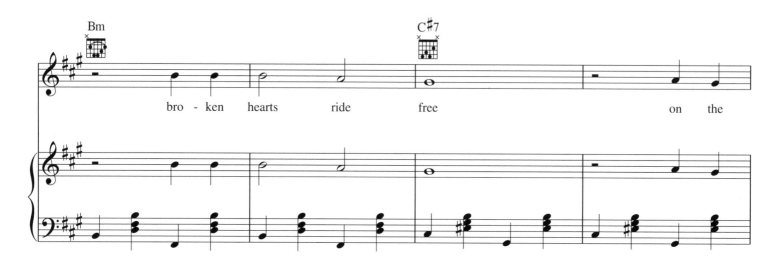

bro-ken hearts ride free on the

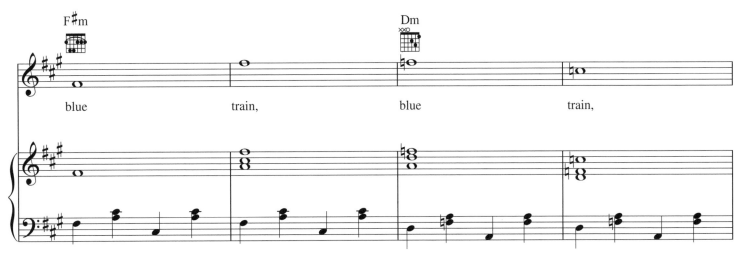

blue   train,   blue   train,

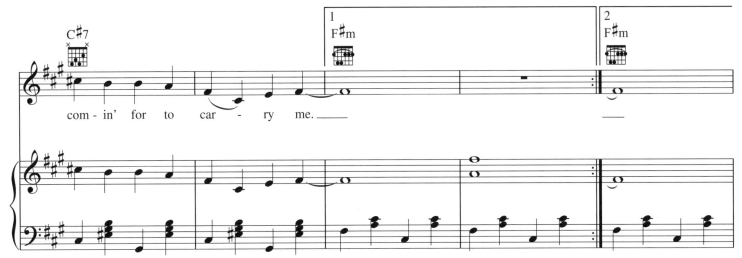

com - in' for to car - ry me. _____

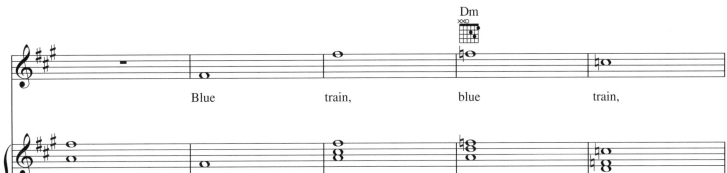

Blue   train,   blue   train,

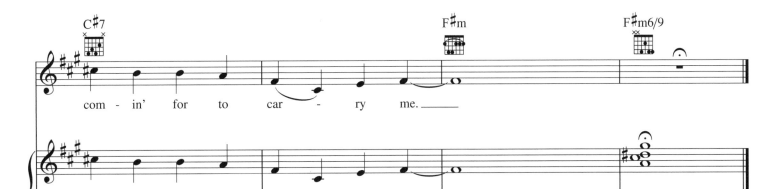

com - in' for to car - ry me. _____

BRINGING MARY HOME

Words and Music by CHAW MANK,
JOE KINGSTON and JOHN DUFFEY

I was driv-in' down a
pulled in to the

lone - ly road ___ on a dark and storm-y night ___
drive - way ___ where ___ she told me to go. ___

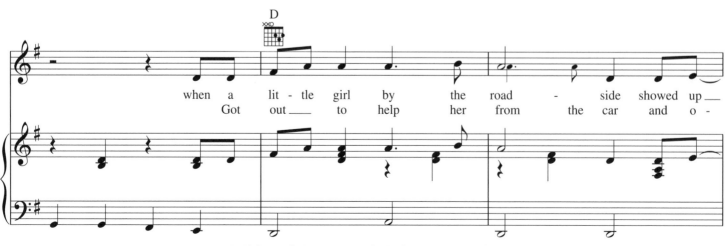

when a lit - tle girl by the road - side showed up ___
Got out ___ to help her from the car and o -

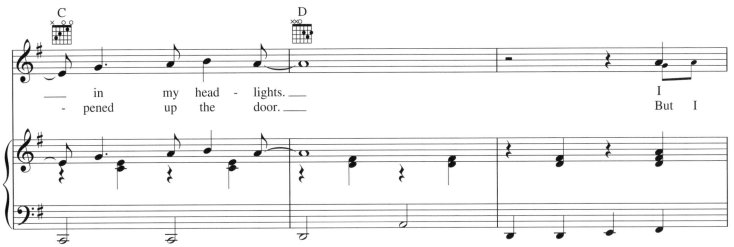

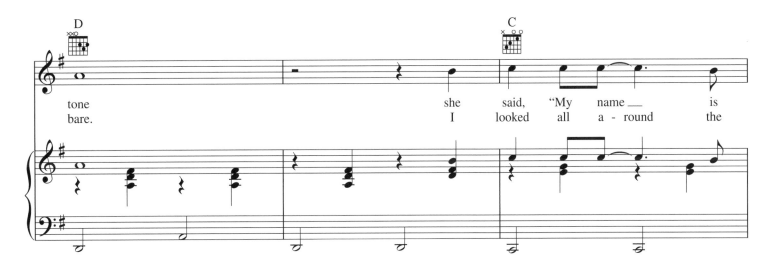

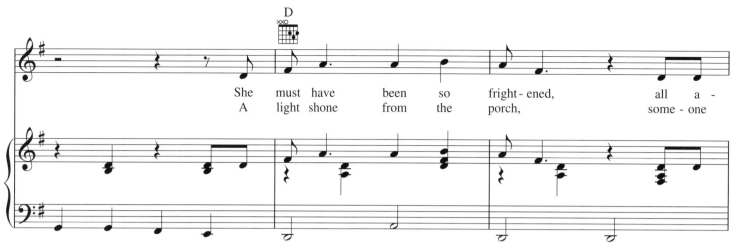

She must have been so fright-ened, all a-
A light shone from the porch, some-one

lone there ____ in the night. ____ There was
o-pened ____ up the door. ____ I

some-thing strange a-bout her, for her face was ____ death-ly
asked a-bout the lit-tle girl her that I was ____ look-ing

white. She sat so pale and
for. The la-dy gen-tly

qui - et in the back seat all a - lone.
smiled _ and brushed a tear a - way.

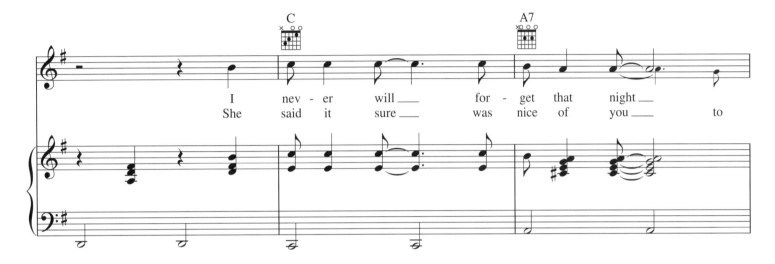

I nev - er will ___ for - get that night ___
She said it sure ___ was nice of you ___ to

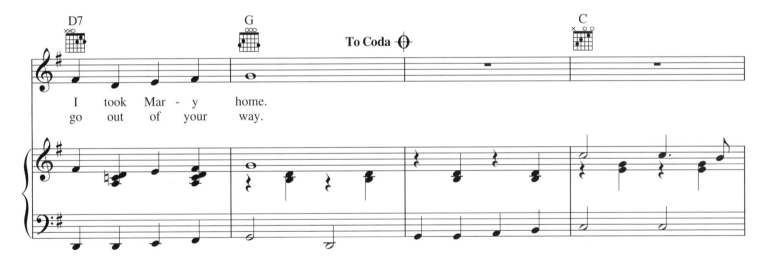

I took Mar - y home.
go out of your way.

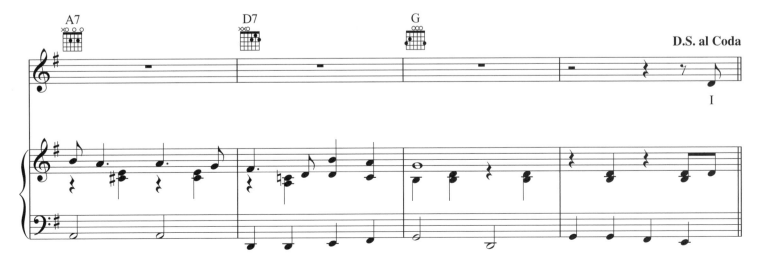

D.S. al Coda

I

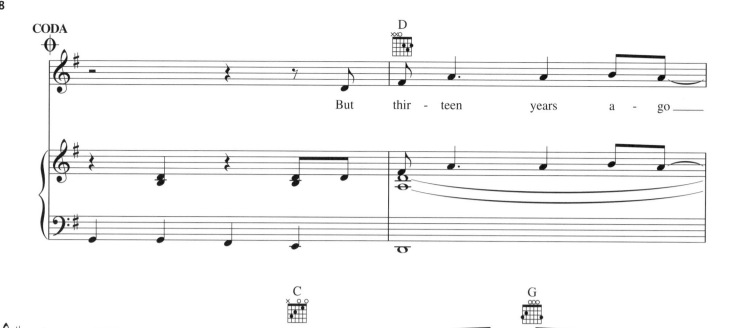

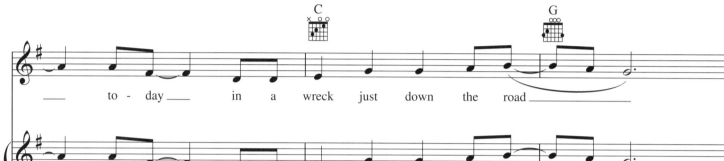

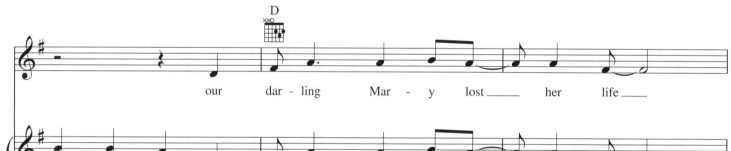

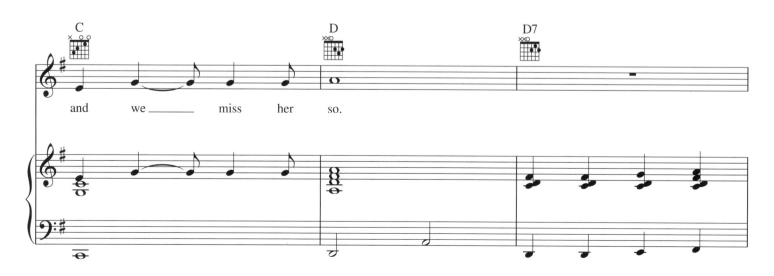

Thank you _____ for your trou - bles and the kind - ness _____ you have

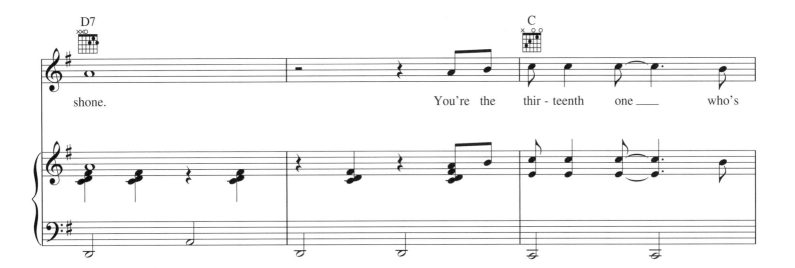

shone. You're the thir - teenth one _____ who's

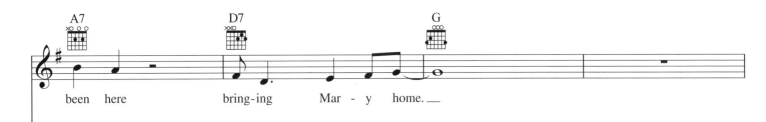

been here bring-ing Mar - y home. __

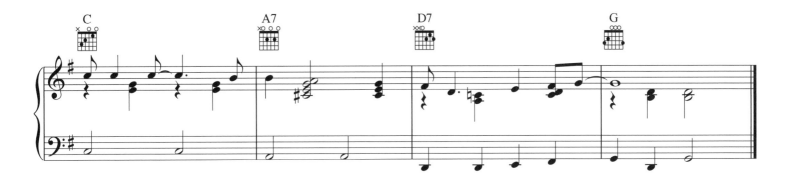

CASH ON THE BARRELHEAD

Words and Music by CHARLES LOUVIN
and IRA LOUVIN

Got in ___ a lit - tle trou - ble at the coun - ty seat. ___
num - ber on a laun - dry slip. ___
jail - house, four ___ days on the

___ road.
Lord, they put me in the jail - house
I had a good - heart - ed jail - er
I was feel - in' might - y hun - gry,

for loaf - in' on the street. ___
with a six - gun hip. ___
I could eats a heav - y load.
When the judge heard the
He let me call long ___
Saw a Grey - hound ___

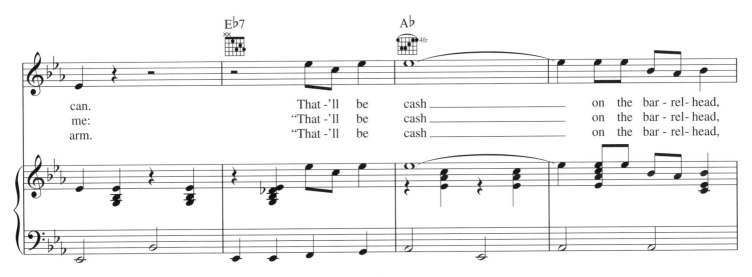

DARK HOLLOW

Words and Music by
BILL BROWNING

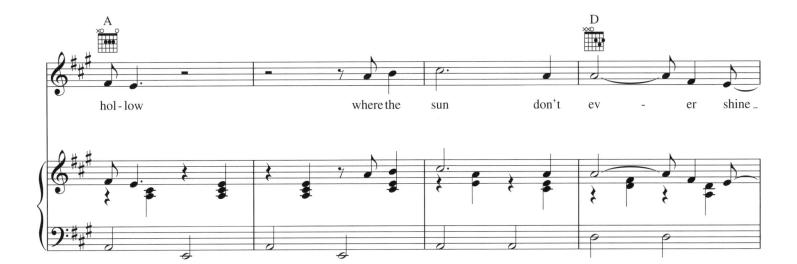

know-in' that ___ you're gone, ___ would cause me to lose ___ my mind. ___
cit - y in a small room with you ___ on my

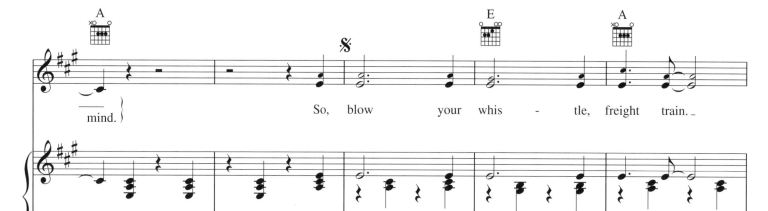

mind. So, blow your whis - tle, freight train. ___

Take me far on down the track. I'm

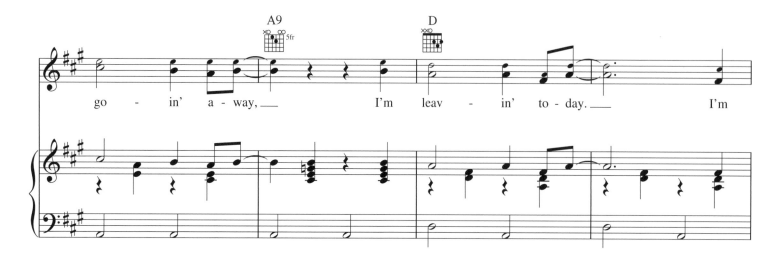

go - in' a - way, ___ I'm leav - in' to - day. ___ I'm

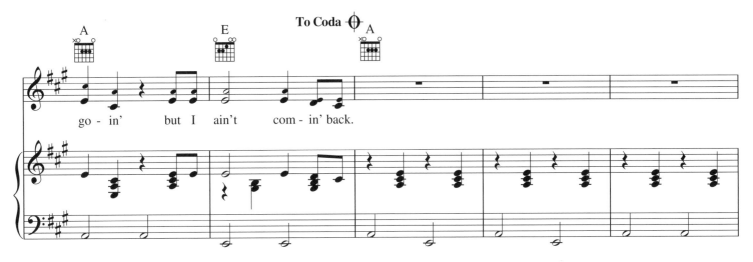

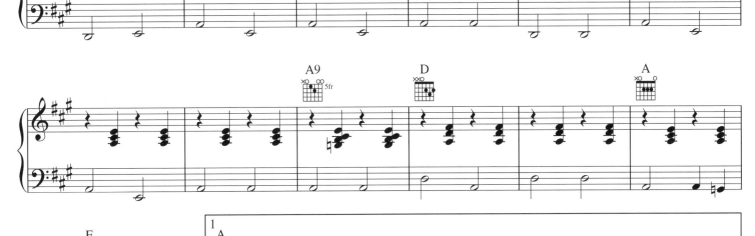

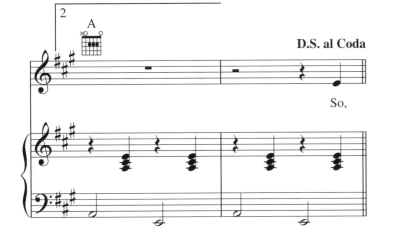

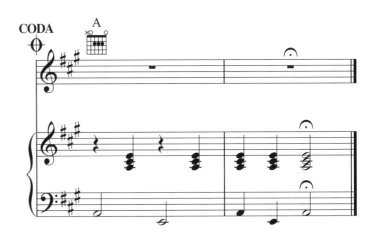

DOIN' MY TIME

Words and Music by
JIMMIE SKINNER

Moderately

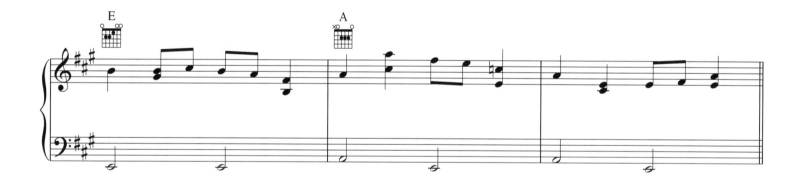

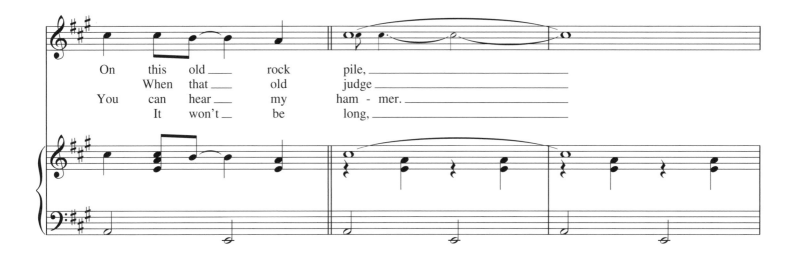

On this old ___ rock pile, ___
When that ___ old judge ___
You can hear ___ my ham - mer. ___
It won't ___ be long, ___

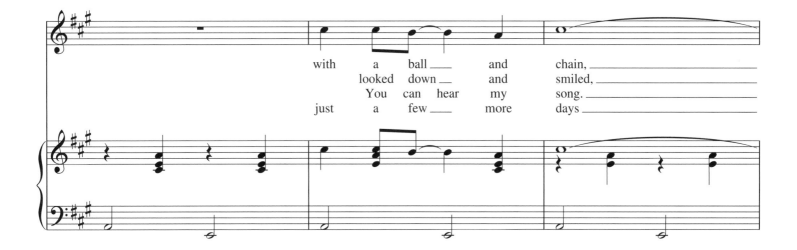

with a ball ___ and chain, ___
looked down ___ and smiled, ___
You can hear my song. ___
just a few ___ more days ___

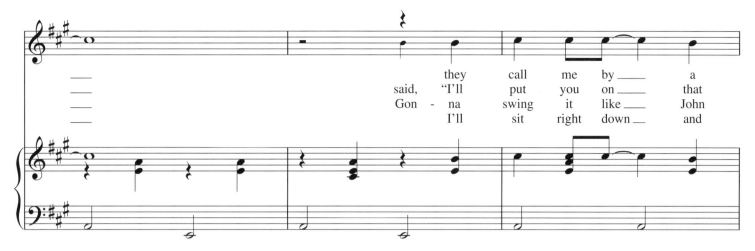

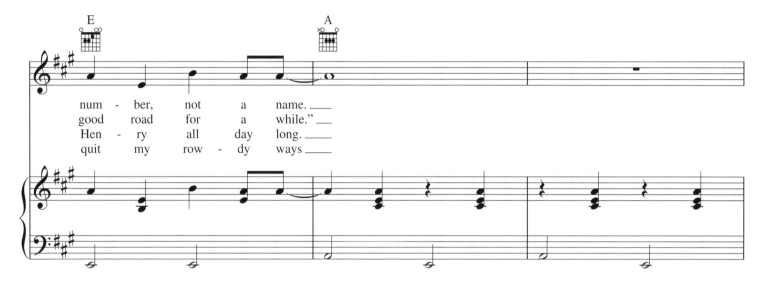

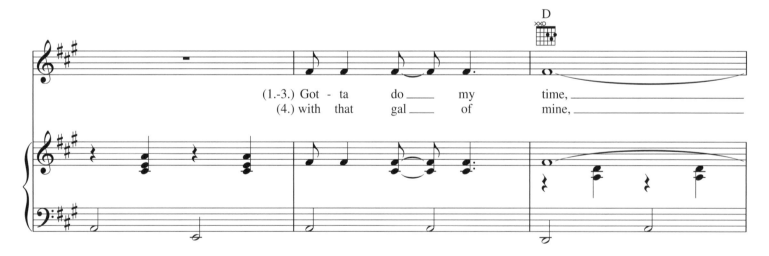

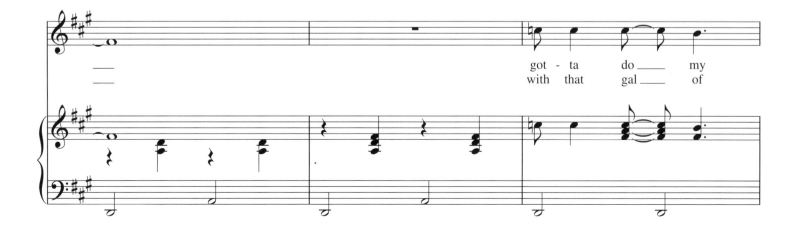

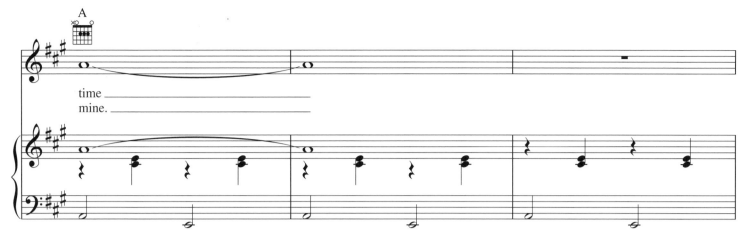

time _____
mine. _____

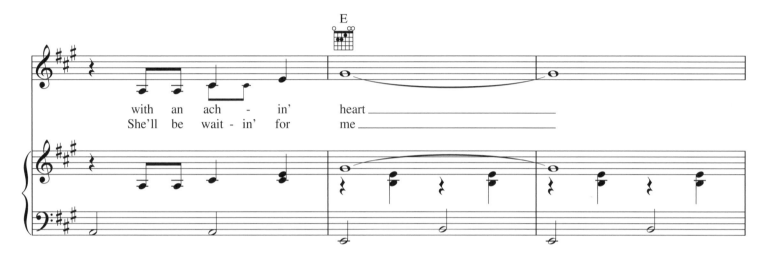

with an ach - in' heart _____
She'll be wait - in' for me _____

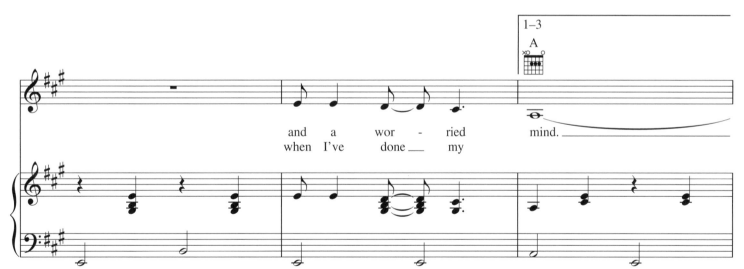

1–3

and a wor - ried mind. _____
when I've done ___ my

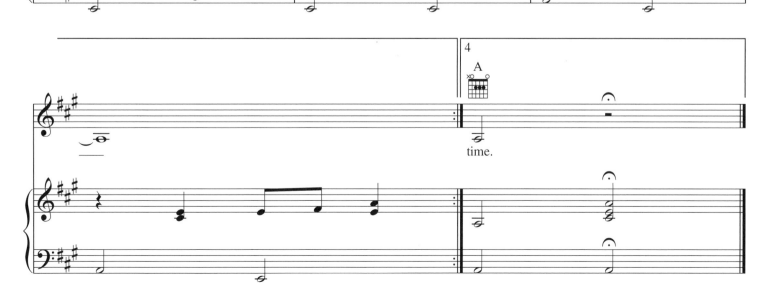

4

time.

DOOLEY

Words and Music by
MITCHELL F. JAYNE

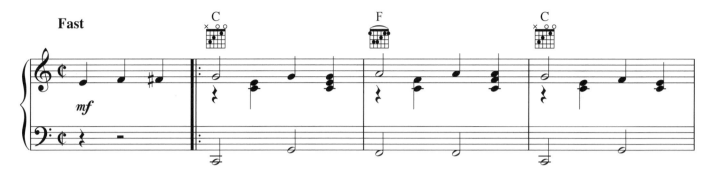

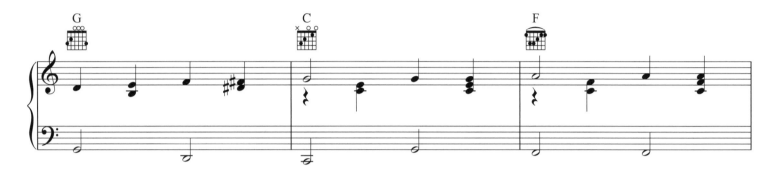

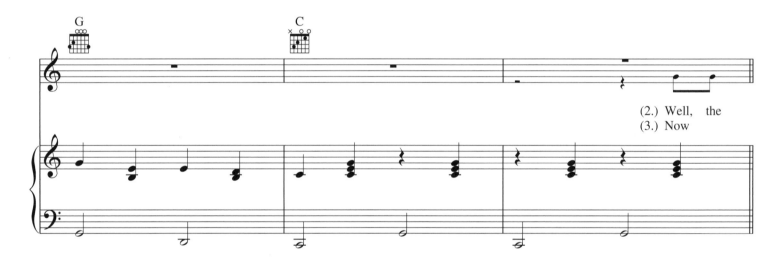

(2.) Well, the
(3.) Now

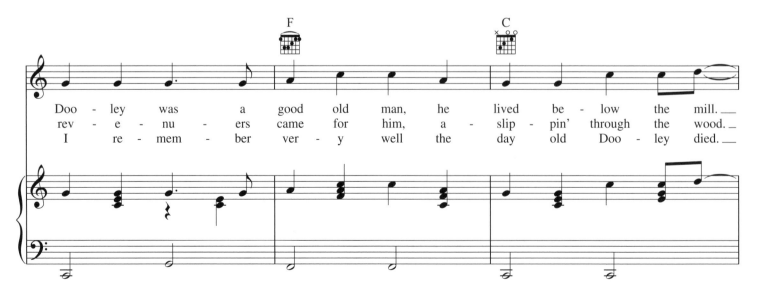

Doo - ley was a good old man, he lived be - low the mill. ___
rev - e - nu - ers came for him, a - slip - pin' through the wood. ___
I re - mem - ber ver - y well the day old Doo - ley died. ___

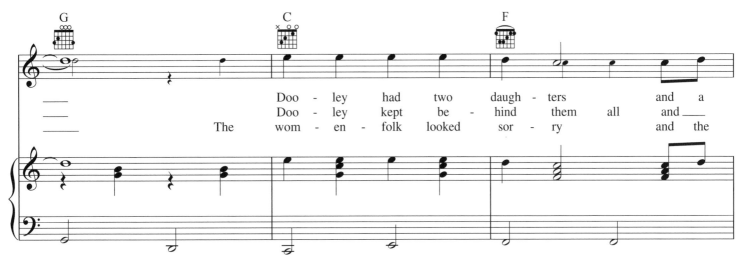

Doo - ley had two daugh - ters and a
Doo - ley kept be - hind them all and
The wom - en - folk looked sor - ry and the

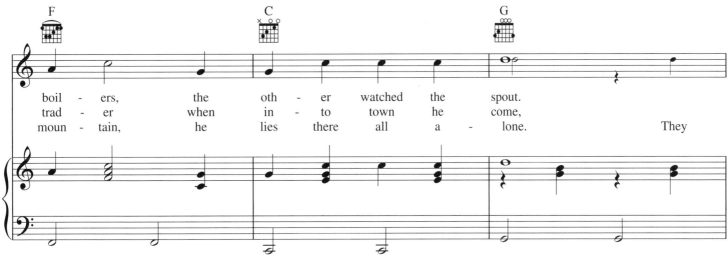

for - ty - gal - lon still. One gal watched the
nev - er lost his goods. Doo - ley was a
men stood 'round and cried. Now Doo - ley's on the

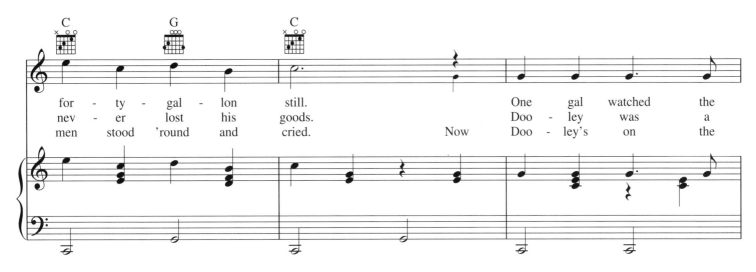

boil - ers, the oth - er watched the spout.
trad - er when in - to town he come,
moun - tain, he lies there all a - lone. They

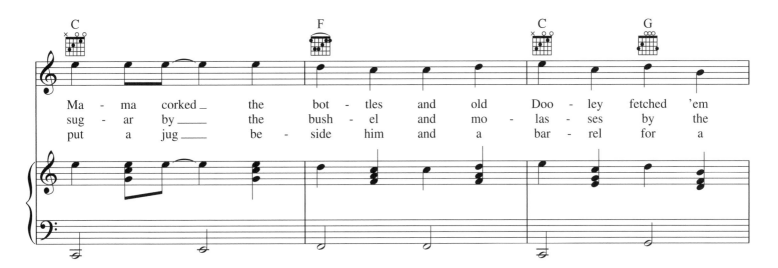

Ma - ma corked the bot - tles and old Doo - ley fetched 'em
sug - ar by the bush - el and old mo - las - ses by the
put a jug be - side him and a bar - rel for a

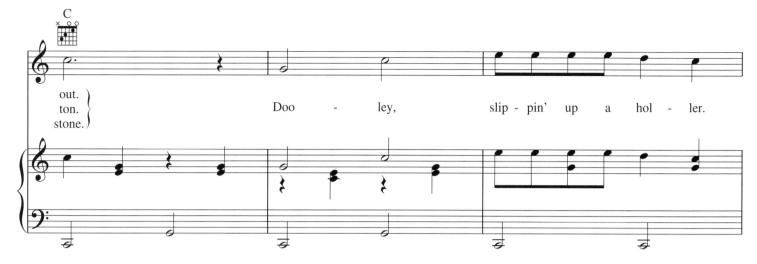

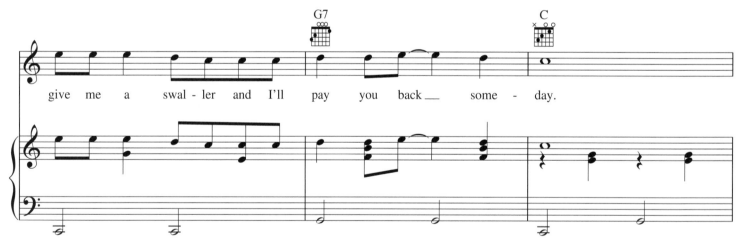

FREEBORN MAN

Words and Music by KEITH ALLISON
and MARK LINDSAY

Freely

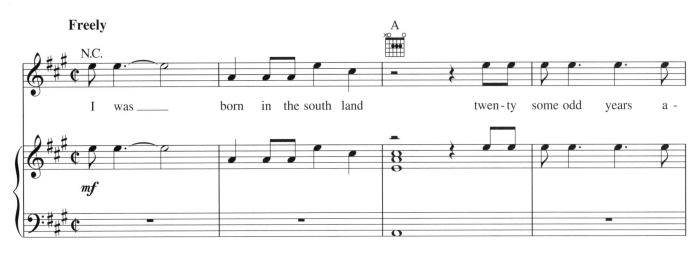

I was ___ born in the south land twen-ty some odd years a-

Moderately fast

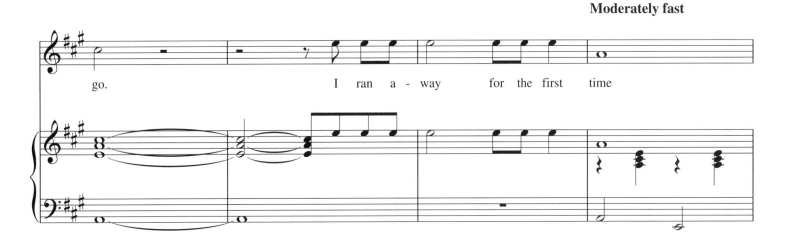

go. I ran a-way for the first time

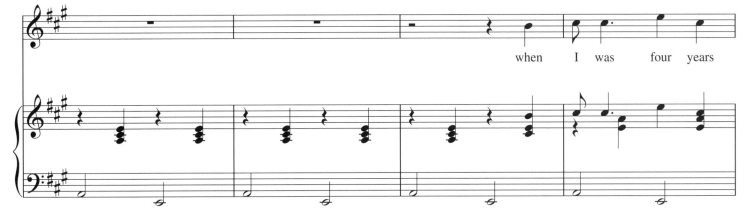

when I was four years

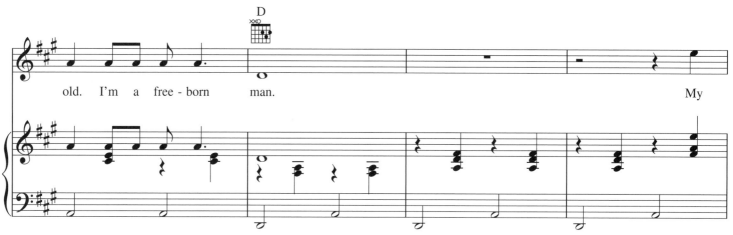

old. I'm a free-born man.   My

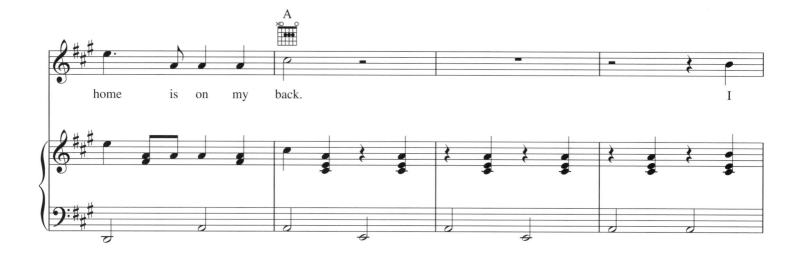

home   is   on   my   back.   I

know ev-'ry inch of high-way,   ev-'ry

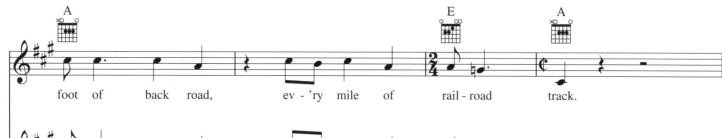

foot   of   back   road,   ev-'ry mile of   rail-road   track.

Got a gal in Cin - cin - na - - ti,
got this worn - out gui - - tar,
may not like my ap - pear - ance

got a wom - an in San An - tone.
I____ car - ry in old tote sack.
and you may__ not like my song.

Said I al - ways loved the girl next door,
Said I hocked it 'bout two hun - dred times.
Said you may not like the way I talk, but,

but an - y - place is home.__
I al - ways get it back.__ I'm a free - born man.
you like the way I'm gone.__

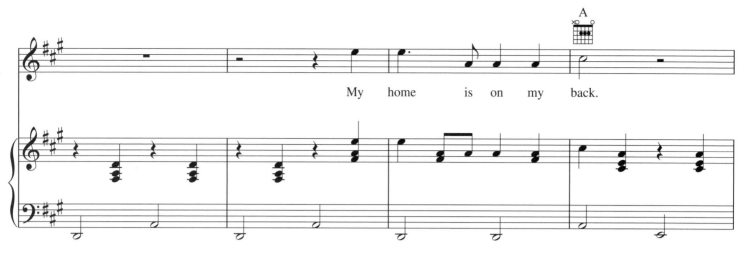

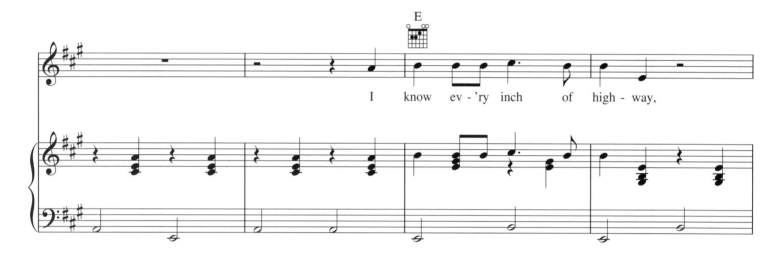

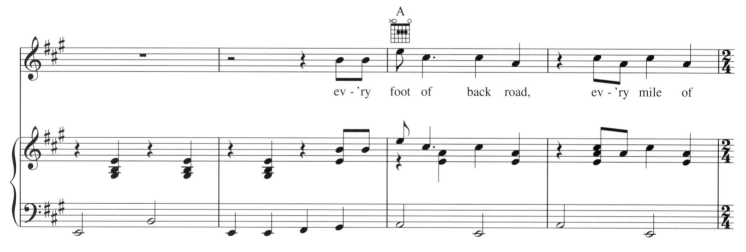

My home is on ___ my back.

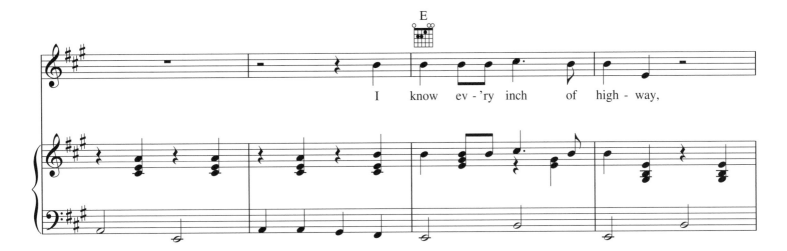

I know ev-'ry inch of high-way,

ev-'ry foot of back road, ev-'ry mile of

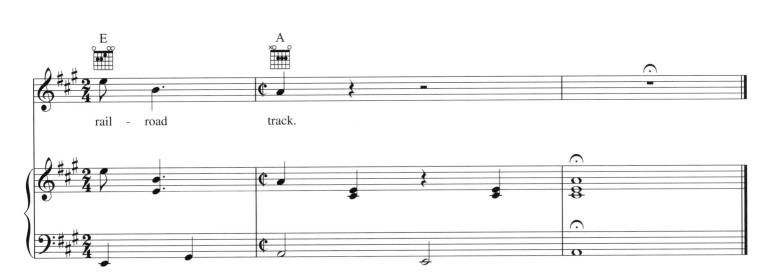

rail - road track.

DOWN THE ROAD

By LESTER FLATT
and EARL SCRUGGS

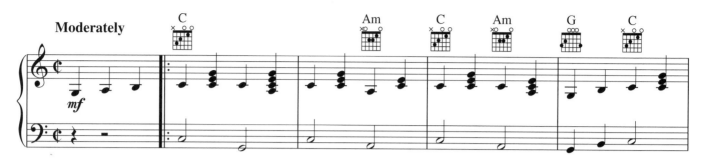

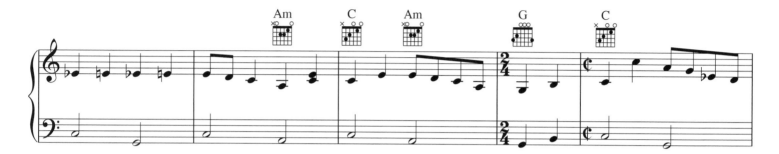

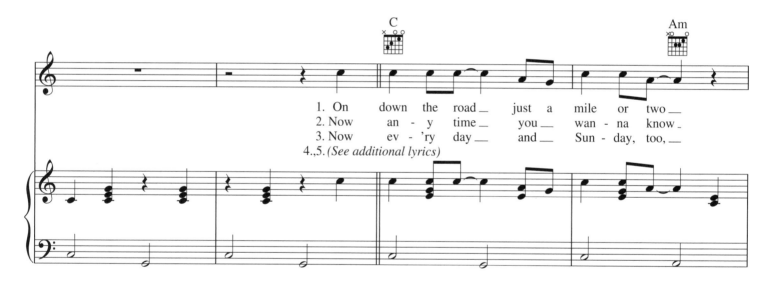

1. On down the road __ just a mile or two __
2. Now an - y time __ you __ wan - na know __
3. Now ev - 'ry day __ and __ Sun - day, too, __
4.,5. *(See additional lyrics)*

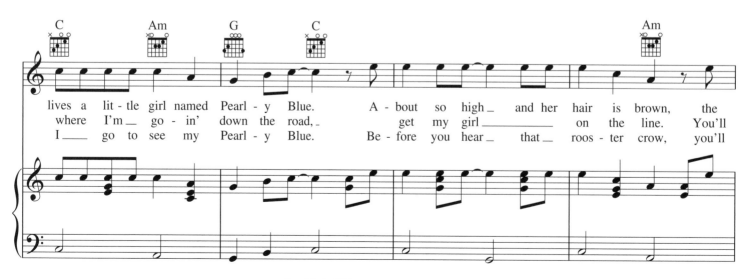

lives a lit - tle girl named Pearl - y Blue. A - bout so high __ and her hair is brown, the
where I'm __ go - in' down the road, __ get my girl _____ on the line. You'll
I __ go to see my Pearl - y Blue. Be - fore you hear __ that __ roos - ter crow, you'll

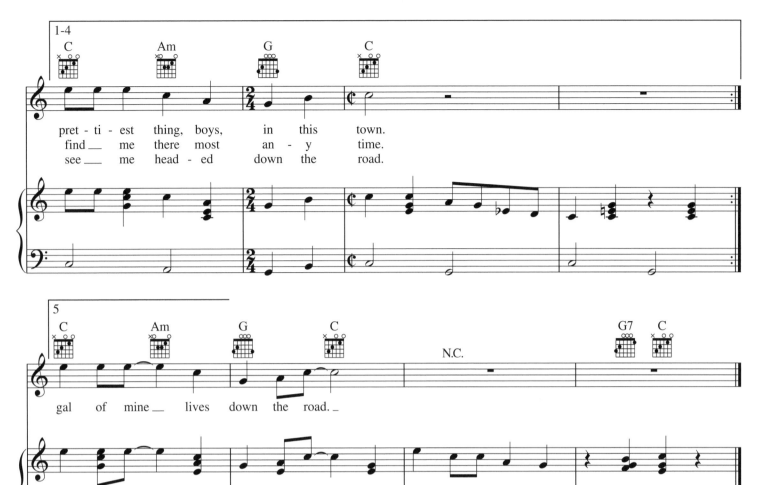

pret - ti - est thing, boys, in this town.
find __ me there most an - y time.
see __ me head - ed down the road.

gal of mine __ lives down the road. _

N.C.

Additional Lyrics

4. Now old man Flatt he owned the farm
    From the hog lot to the barn.
    From the barn to the rail
    He made his living by carrying the mail.

5. Now every time I get the blues
    I walk the soles right off my shoes.
    I don't know why I love her so
    That gal of mine lives down the road.

FOGGY MOUNTAIN TOP

Words and Music by A.P. CARTER,
MAYBELLE CARTER and SARA CARTER

Not too fast

If   I   was   on   some

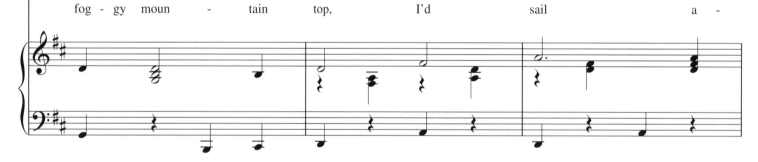

fog- gy moun- tain top,   I'd   sail   a-

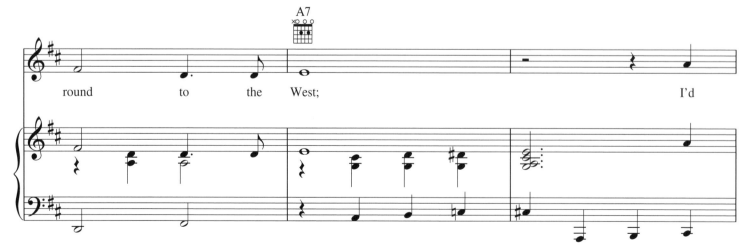

round   to   the   West;   I'd

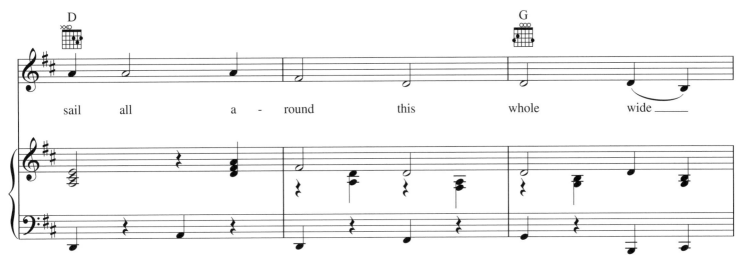

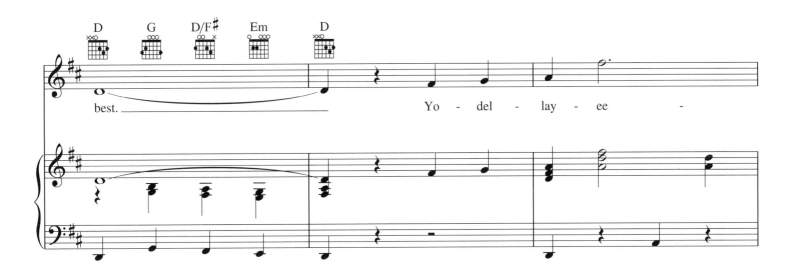
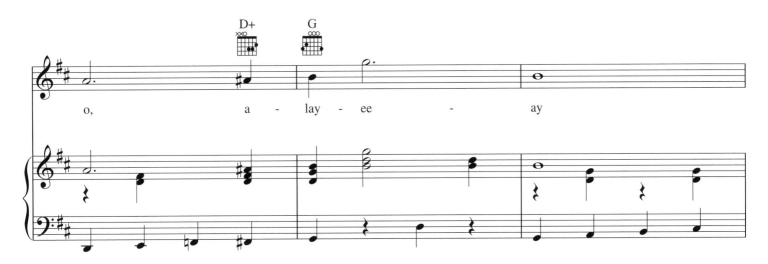

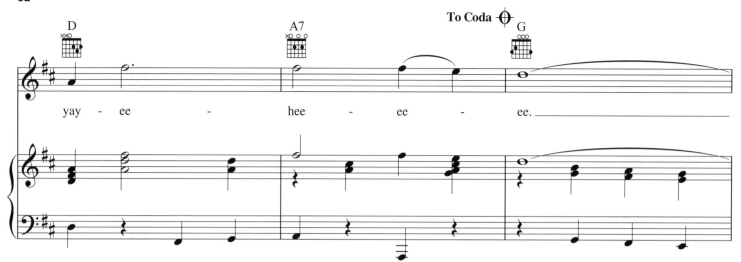

yay - ee - hee - ee - ee.

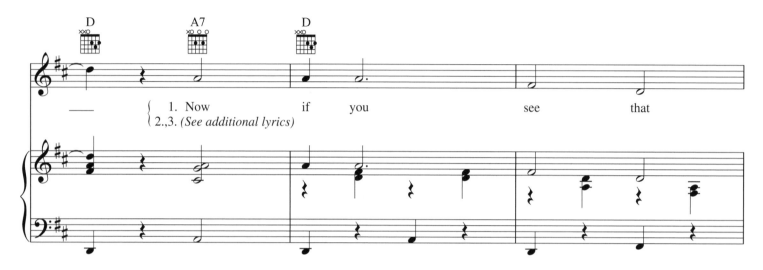

— 1. Now if you see that
2.,3. *(See additional lyrics)*

girl of _____ mine, there's some - thing I want you to

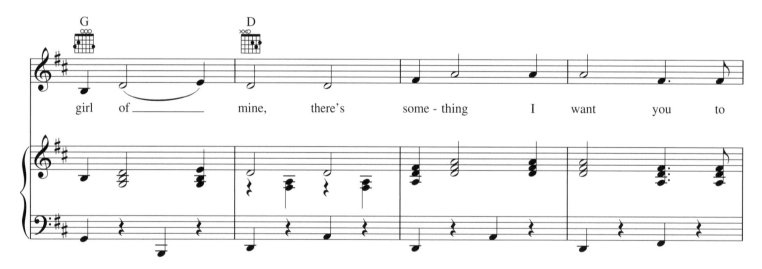

tell her. Tell her not to be

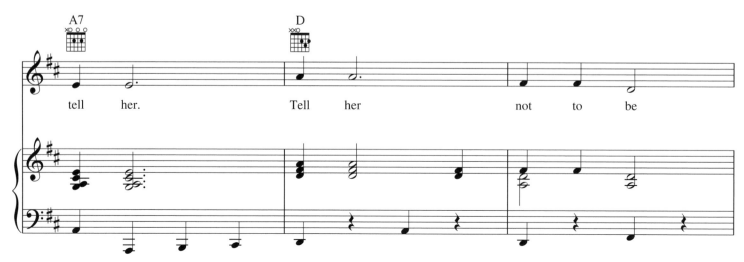

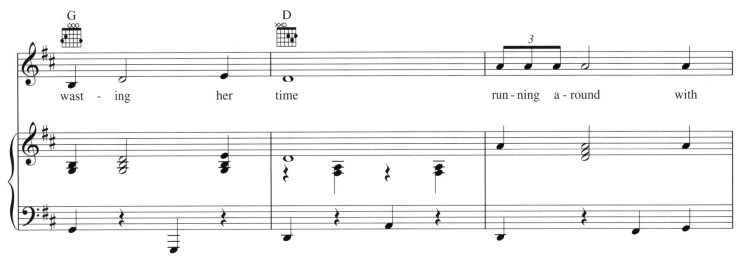

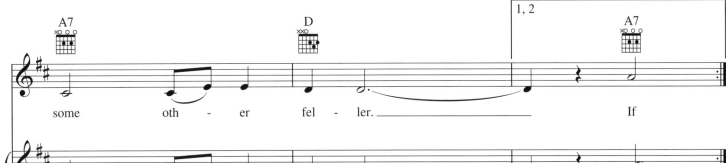

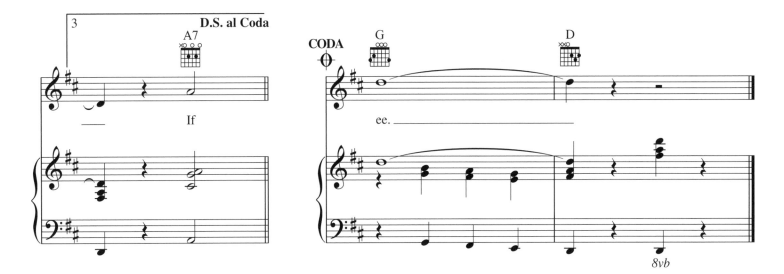

Additional Lyrics

2. Oh, she's caused me to weep and she's caused me to moan,
   She caused me to leave my home;
   The lonesome pines and good old times,
   I'm on my way back home.

3. Oh, if I'd only listened to what my mama said,
   I would not have been there today
   Lying around this old jail cell,
   Just a-weeping my poor life away.

FOOTPRINTS IN THE SNOW

Words and Music by
RUPERT JONES

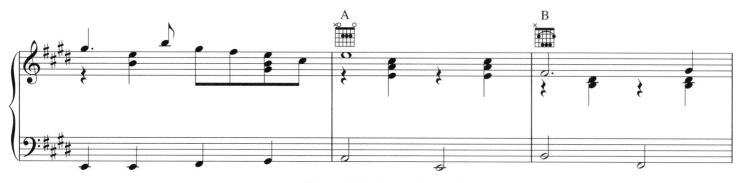

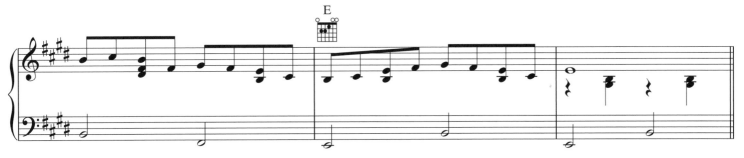

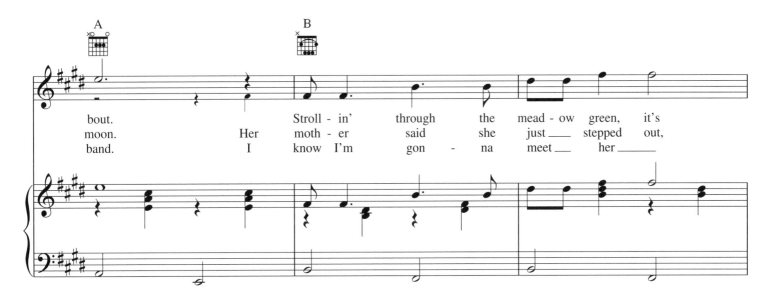

Some folks like the sum - mer - time _____ when they can walk a -
I dropped in to see _____ her, _____ there was a big, round
Now she's up in heav - en, _____ she's with the an - gel

bout. Stroll - in' through the mead - ow green, it's
moon. Her moth - er said she just _____ stepped out,
band. I know I'm gon - na meet _____ her _____

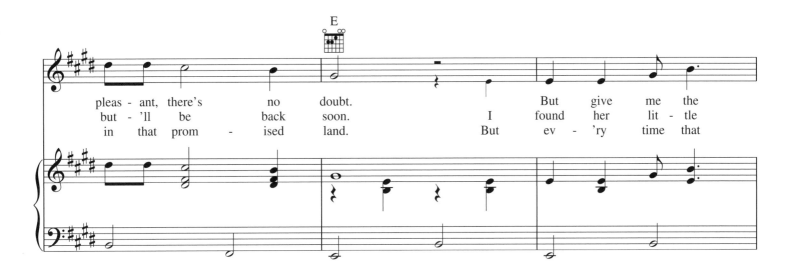

pleas - ant, there's no doubt. But give me the
but - 'll be back soon. I found her lit - tle
in that prom - ised land. But ev - 'ry time that

win - ter - time when the snow is on the ground, for I
foot - prints and ___ traced 'em through the snow. I
snow ___ falls, it ___ brings back mem - o - ries, for I

found her when the snow was on the ground.
found her when the snow was on the ground.
found her when the snow was on the ground.

I traced ___ her lit - tle foot - prints in the

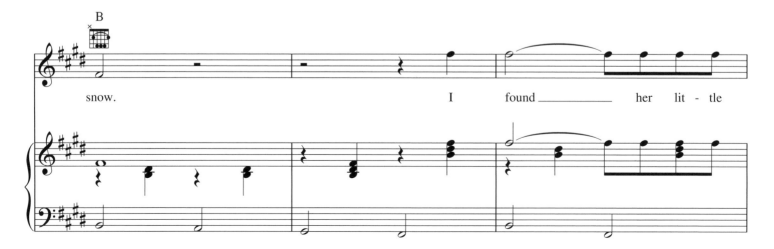

snow. I found ___ her lit - tle

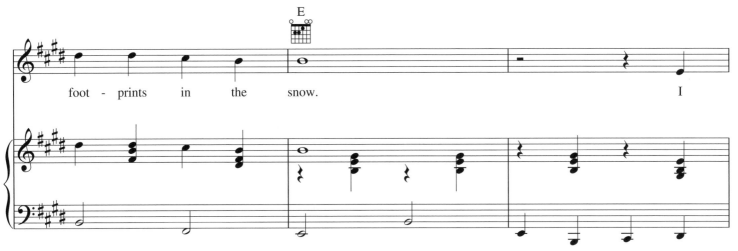

foot - prints in the snow. I

bless that hap - py day when Nel - lie lost her

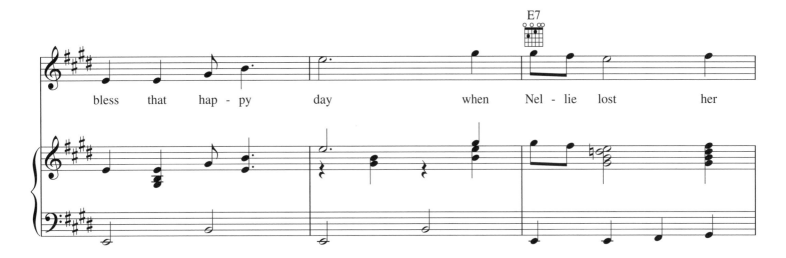

way, for I found her when the snow was on the

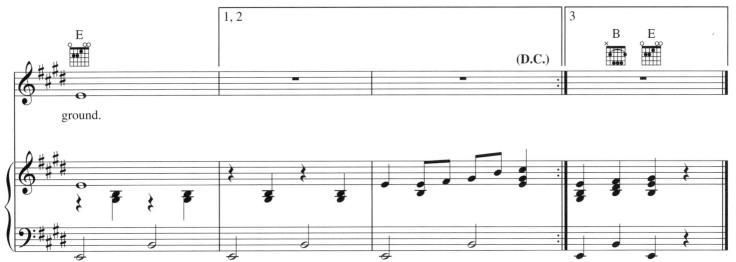

ground.

FOX ON THE RUN

Words and Music by
TONY HAZZARD

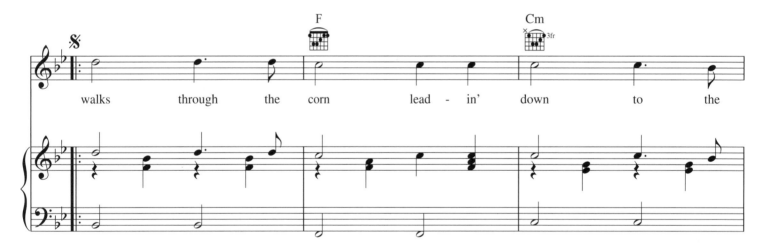

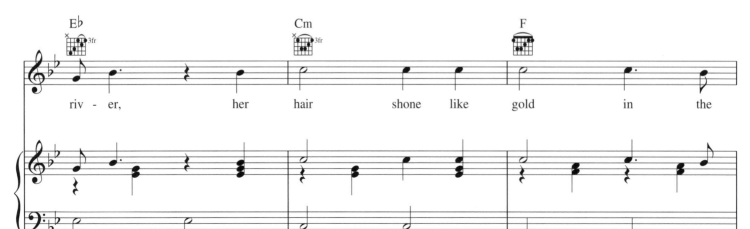

hot morn - in' sun. She took all the

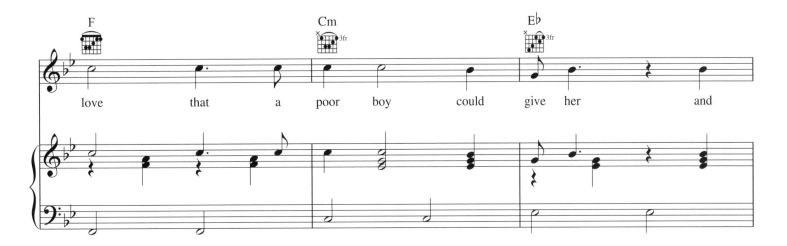

love that a poor boy could give her and

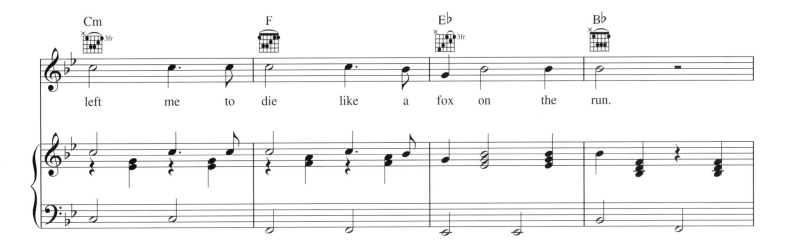

left me to die like a fox on the run.

Like a fox, _____ like a fox, _____ like a fox, _

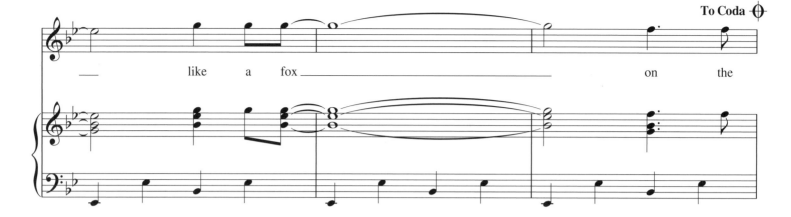

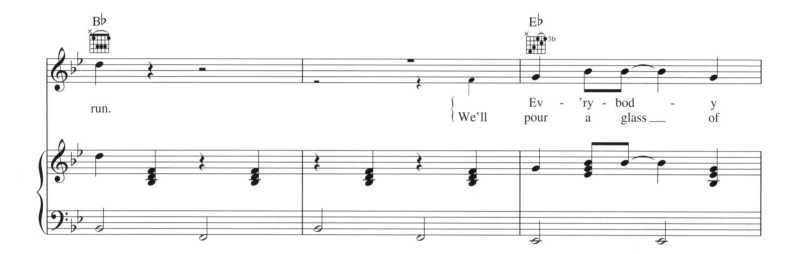

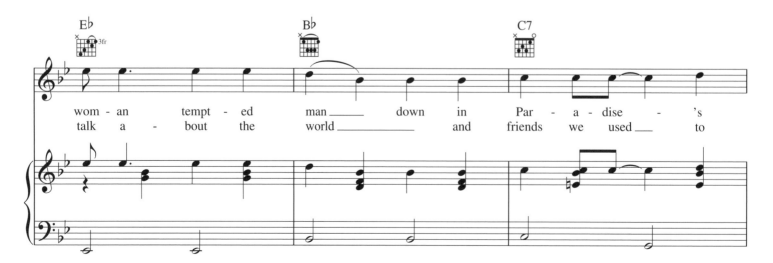

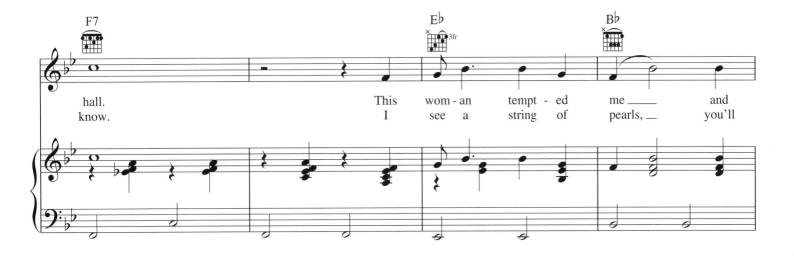

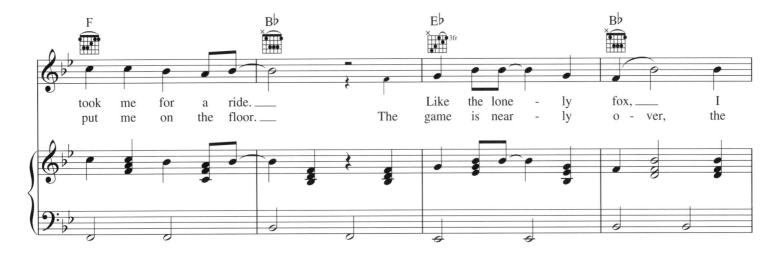

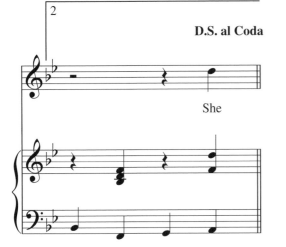

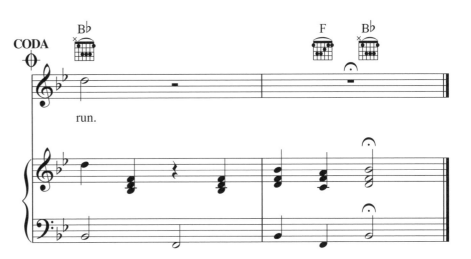

GINSENG SULLIVAN

Words and Music by
NORMAN BLAKE

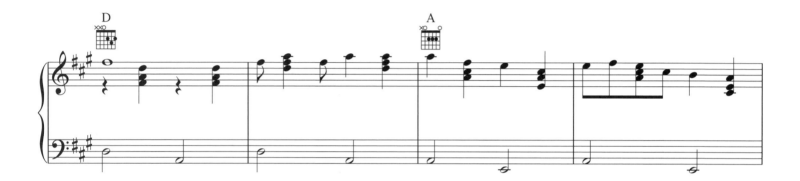

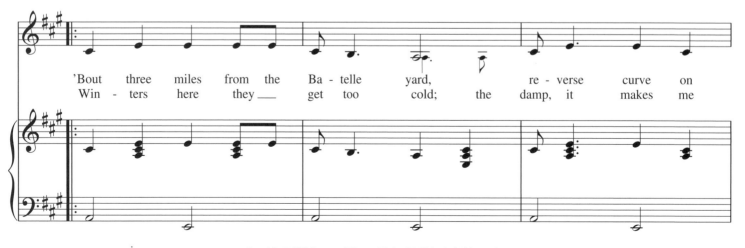

'Bout three miles from the Ba - telle yard, re - verse curve on
Win - ters here they ___ get too cold; the damp, it makes me

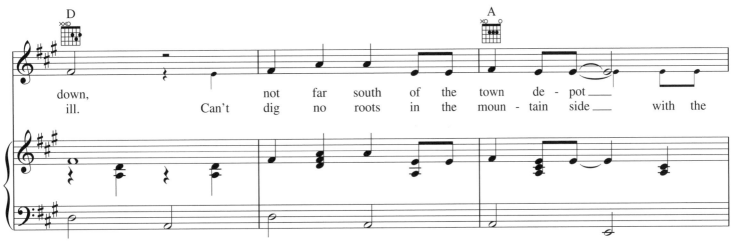

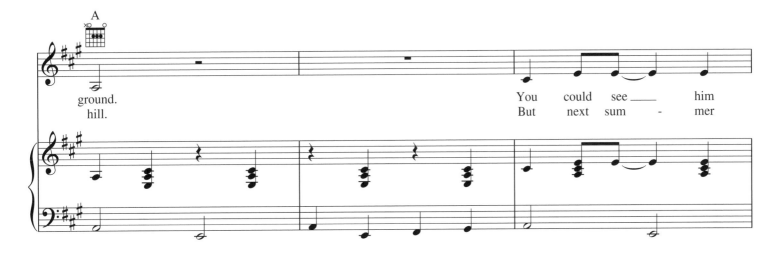

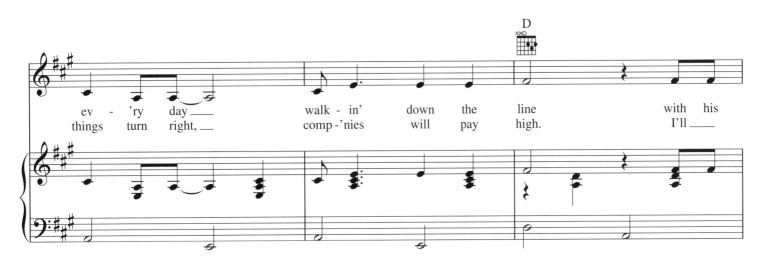

old brown sack a-cross his back, __ long hair down be-hind, __
make e-nough mon-ey to pay my bills, __ bid these moun-tains good-

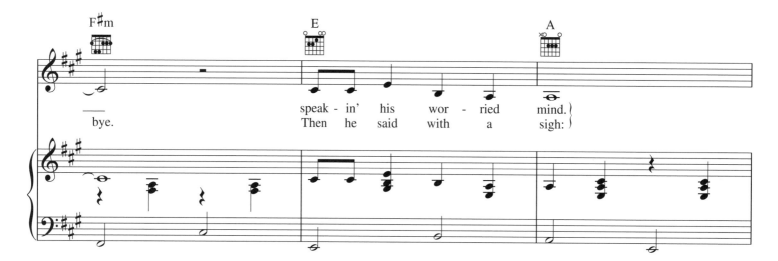

speak-in' his wor-ried mind.)
Then he said with a sigh: }

__ bye.

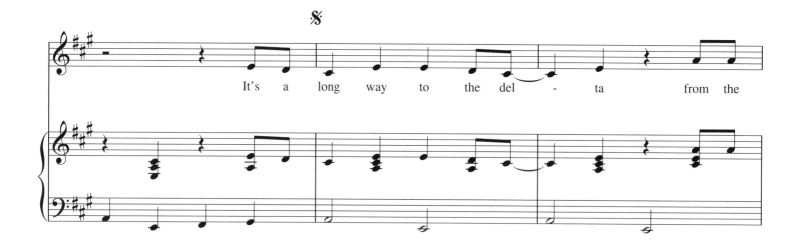

It's a long way to the del - ta from the

North Geor-gia hills, __ and a tote sack full of gin-

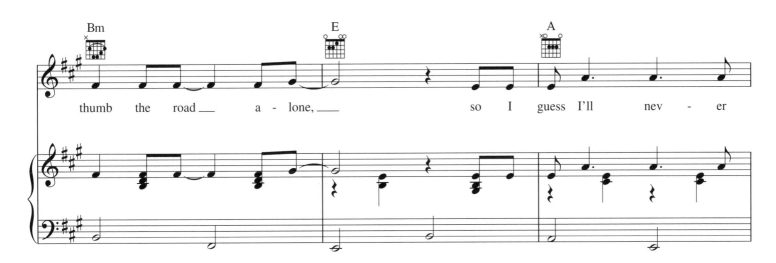

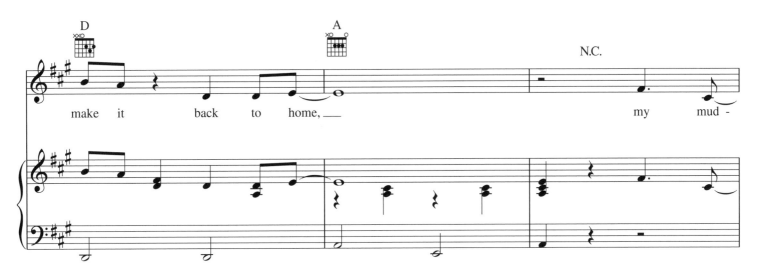

HIGH ON A MOUNTAIN TOP

Words and Music by
OLA BELLE REED

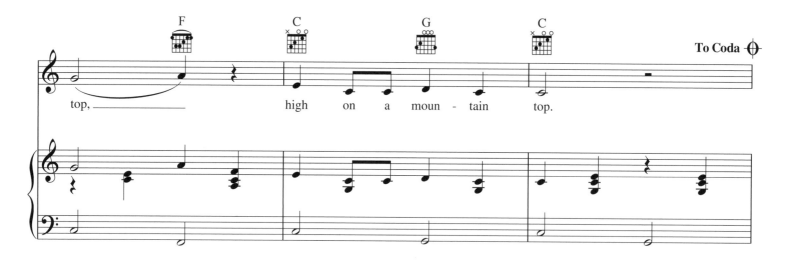

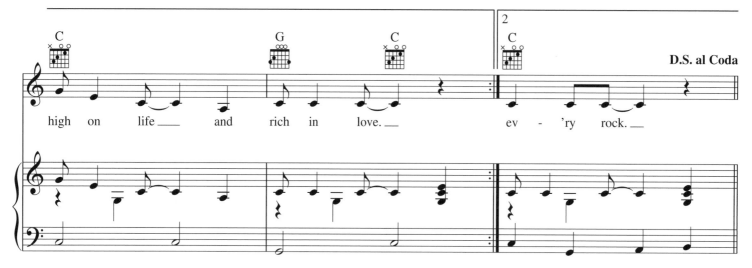

high on life ___ and rich in love. ___

ev - 'ry rock. ___

D.S. al Coda

CODA

Well, we lay on our backs and we count the stars, ___ 'cause

up here, folks, ___ heav-en's not that far. ___

High ___ on a

moun - tain top ___ we live, we love and we laugh a lot. ___

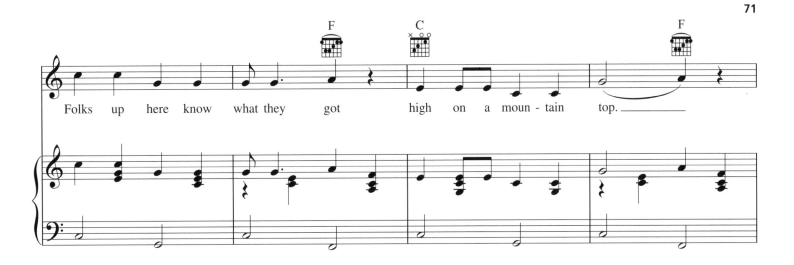

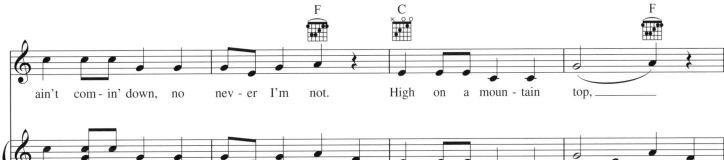

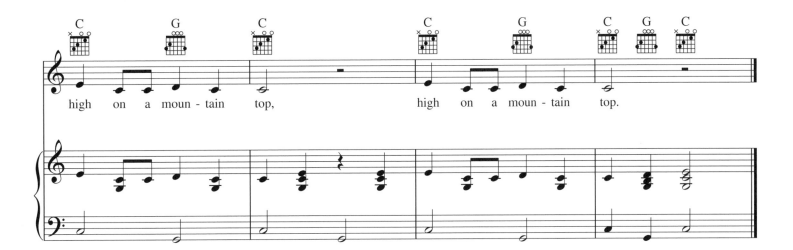

GREEN LIGHT ON THE SOUTHERN

Words and Music by
NORMAN BLAKE

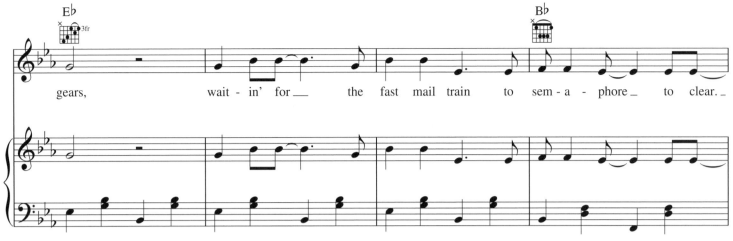

gears, wait - in' for ___ the fast mail train to sem - a - phore ___ to clear. ___

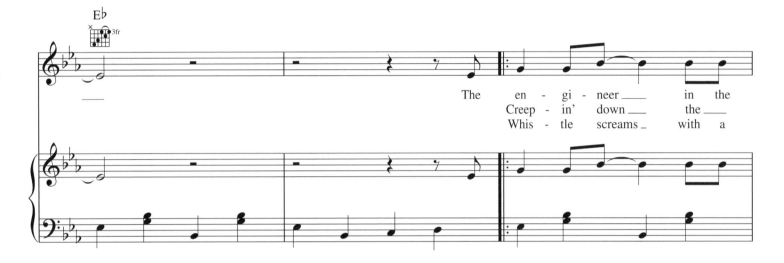

The en - gi - neer ___ in the
Creep - in' down ___ the ___
Whis - tle screams ___ with a

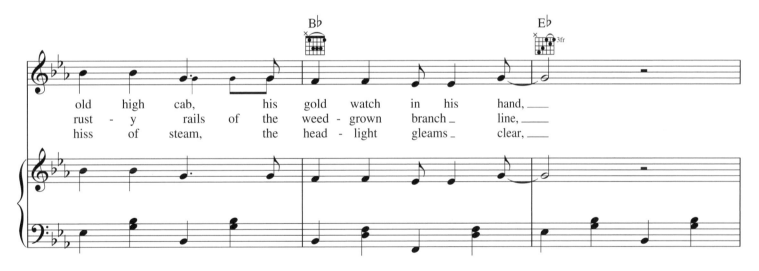

old high cab, his gold watch in his hand, ___
rust - y rails of the weed - grown branch ___ line, ___
hiss of steam, the head - light gleams ___ clear, ___

look - in' at ___ the wa - ter glass and let - tin' down the sand, ___
sec - tion hous - es gray and white by the yard ___ lim - it sign, ___
driv - er rolls on the green and go, get - tin' might - y near, ___

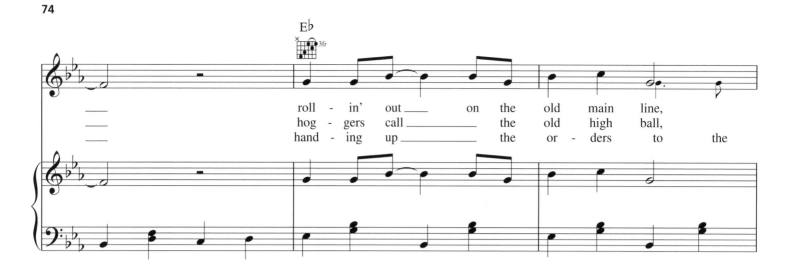

roll - in' out ___ on the old main line,
hog - gers call _____ the old high ball,
hand - ing up _____ the or - ders to the

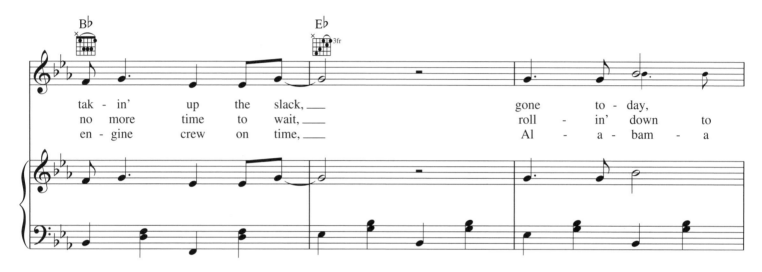

tak - in' up the slack, ___ gone to - day,
no more time to wait, ___ roll - in' down to
en - gine crew on time, ___ Al - a - bam - a

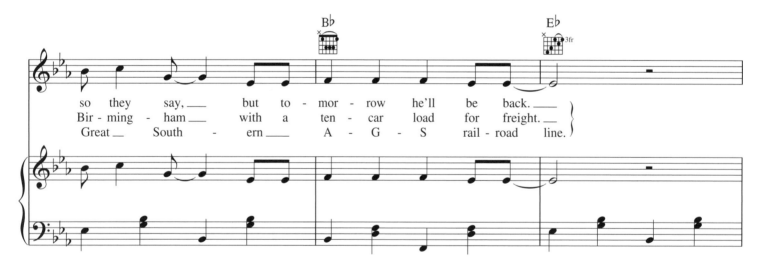

so they say, ___ but to - mor - row he'll be back. ___
Bir - ming - ham ___ with a ten - car load for freight. ___
Great ___ South - ern ___ A - G - S rail - road line.

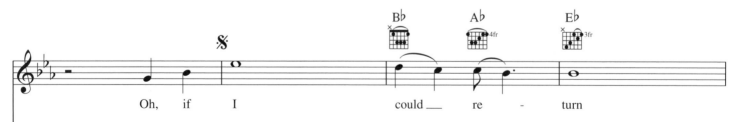

Oh, if I could ___ re - turn

HEAD OVER HEELS IN LOVE WITH YOU

(I'm Head over Heels in Love)

Words and Music by
LESTER FLATT

be - cause I'm head o - ver heels in love with you.

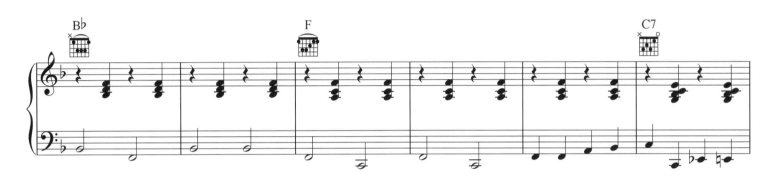

Ev - ry   I'm feel - in' so blue   I
Oh, I'd
Oh, the

don't know what to do ___ be - cause I'm head o - ver heels in love with you.

HOW MOUNTAIN GIRLS CAN LOVE

Words and Music by
RUBY RAKES

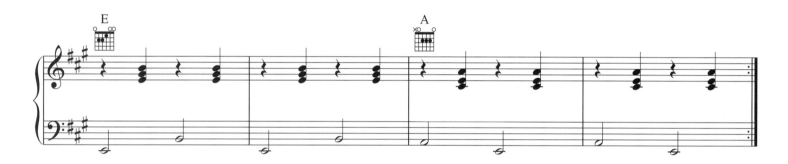

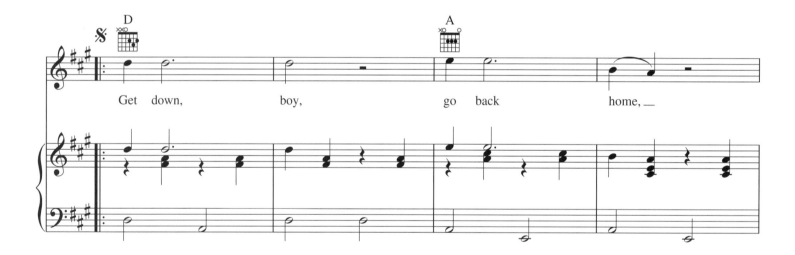

Get down, boy, go back home, —

back to the girl you love.

Treat her right, nev - er wrong.

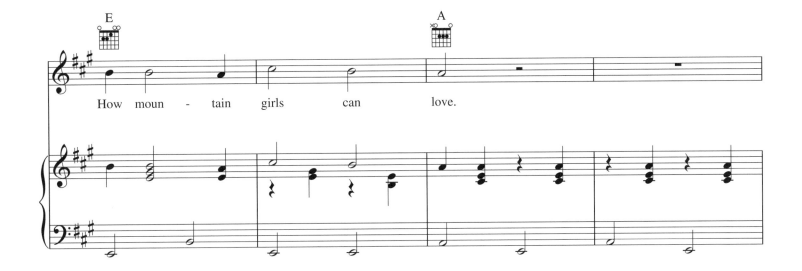

How moun - tain girls can love.

To Coda ⊕

Rid - in' the night in the
Re - mem - ber the night _____ we

high, cold wind _____ on the trail of the
strolled down the lane? _____ Our hearts _____ were

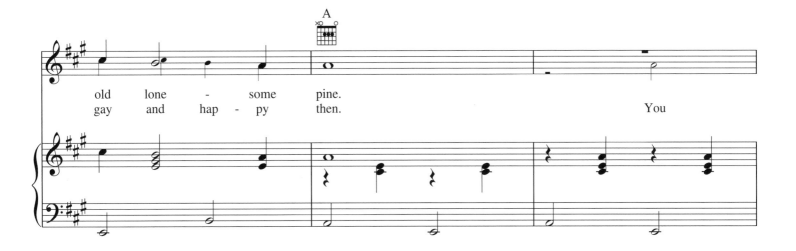

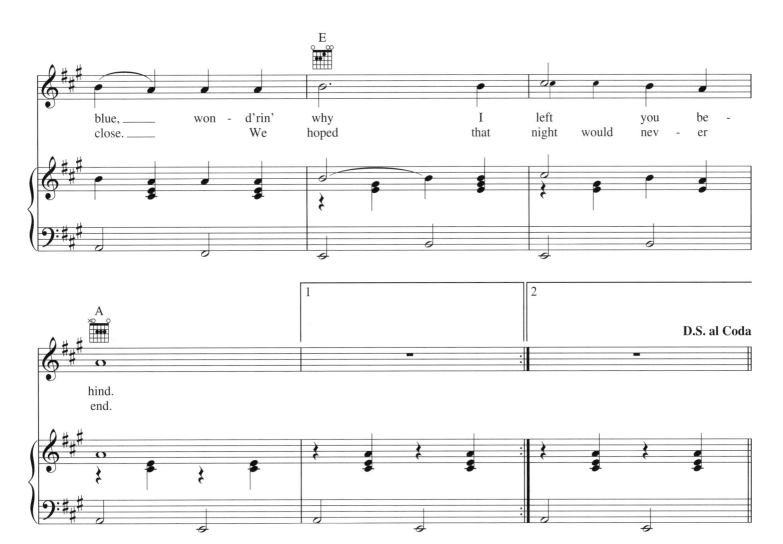

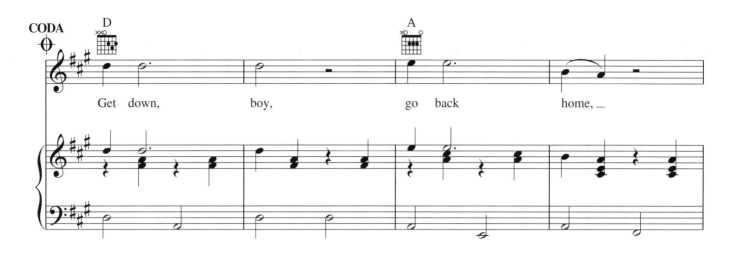

Get down, boy, go back home, __

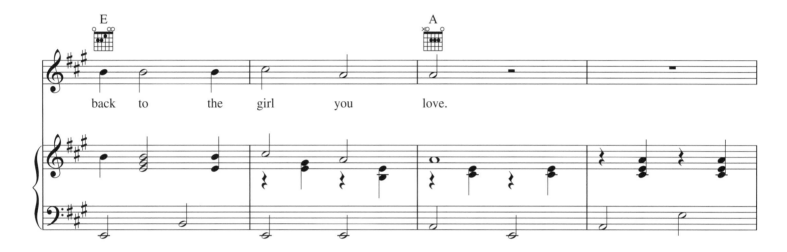

back to the girl you love.

Treat her right, nev - er wrong. __

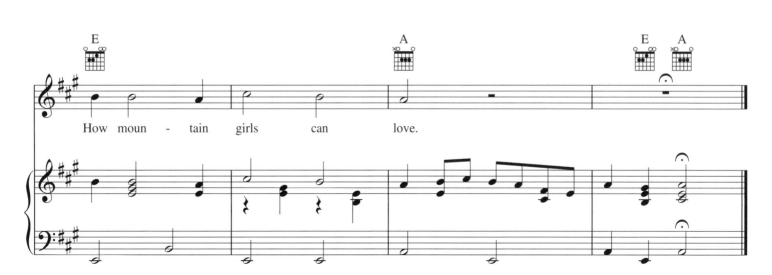

How moun - tain girls can love.

I AM A MAN OF CONSTANT SORROW

featured in O BROTHER, WHERE ART THOU?

Words and Music by
CARTER STANLEY

sor - row. _____ I've seen trou - ble all ___ my
trou - ble, _____ no pleas - ure here _____ on earth I've
lov - er, _____ I nev - er ex - pect _____ to see you a -
val - ley _____ for man - y years _____ where I ___ may lay,
stran - ger; _____ my face ___ you nev - er will see ___ no

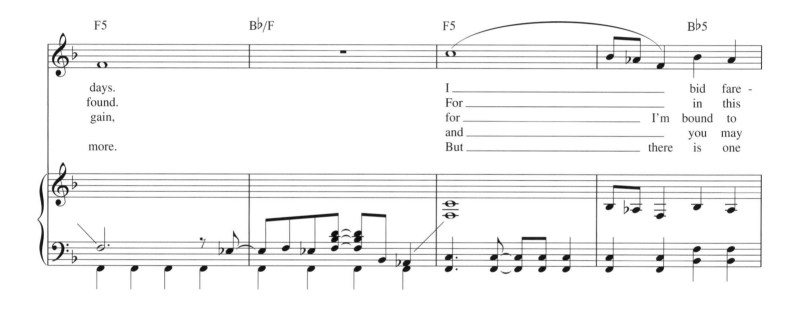

days.
found.
gain,
more.

I _____ bid fare -
For _____ in this
for _____ I'm bound to
and _____ you may
But _____ there is one

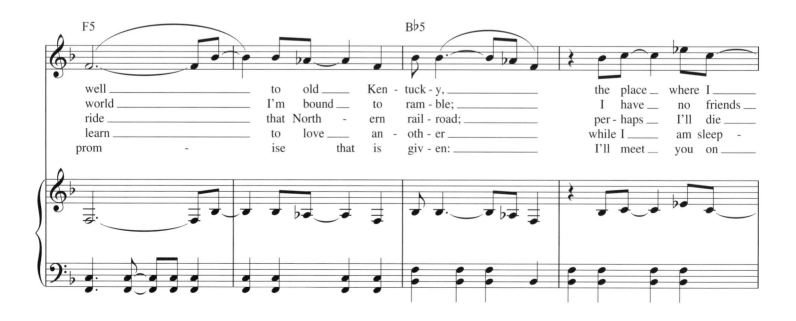

well _____ to old ___ Ken - tuck - y, _____ the place ___ where I _____
world _____ I'm bound ___ to ram - ble; _____ I have ___ no friends _____
ride _____ that North - ern rail - road; _____ per - haps ___ I'll die _____
learn _____ to love ___ an - oth - er _____ while I ___ am sleep -
prom - ise that is giv - en: _____ I'll meet ___ you on _____

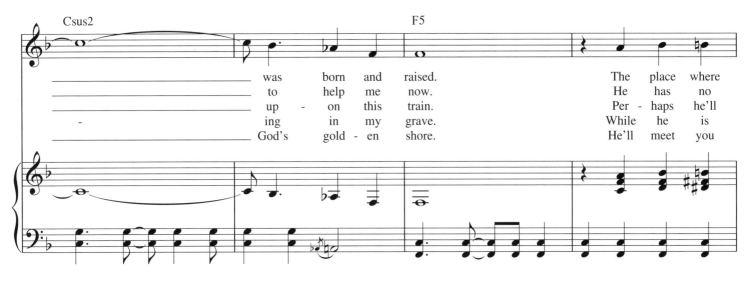

was born and raised. The place where
to help me now. He has no
up - on this train. Per - haps he'll
ing in my grave. While he is
God's gold - en shore. He'll meet you

he _____ was born and raised.
friends _____ to help him now.
die _____ up - on this train.
sleep - ing in his grave.
on _____ God's gold - en

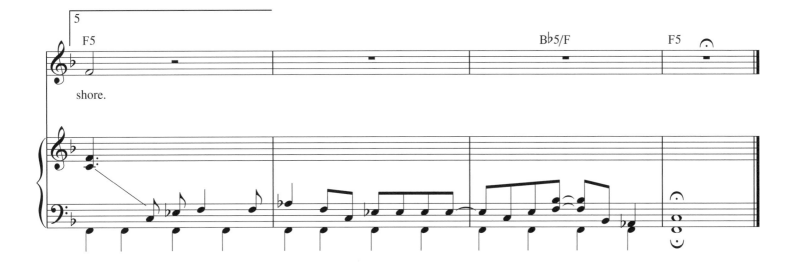

shore.

I AIN'T GOIN' TO WORK TOMORROW

Words and Music by A.P. CARTER,
LESTER FLATT and EARL SCRUGGS

Moderately

I'm   a-
Well,   she
Well,   I
Well,   I

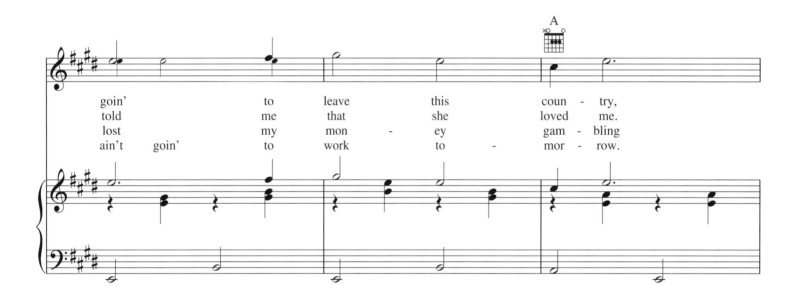

goin'   to   leave   this   coun - try,
told   me   that   she   loved   me.
lost   my   mon - ey   gam - bling
ain't   goin'   to   work   to - mor - row.

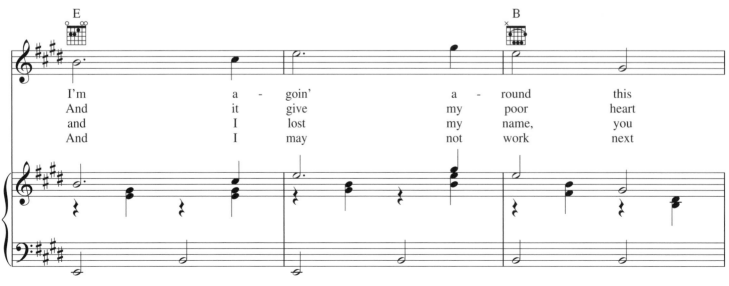

I'm   a - goin'   a - round   this
And   it   give   my   poor   heart
and   I   lost   my   name,   you
And   I   may   not   work   next

I'LL FLY AWAY

Words and Music by
ALBERT E. BRUMLEY

Moderately fast Country

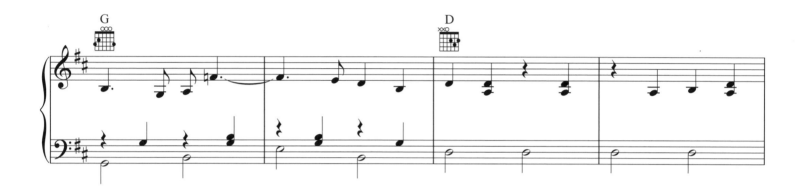

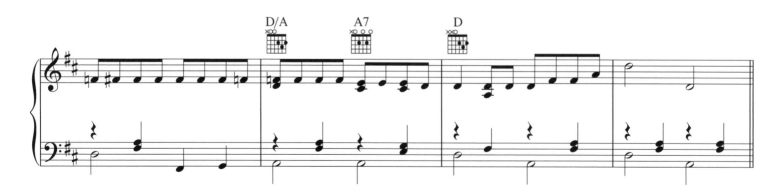

way.

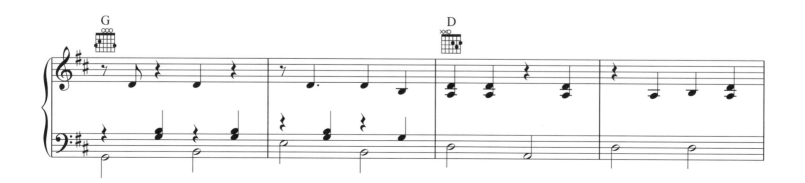

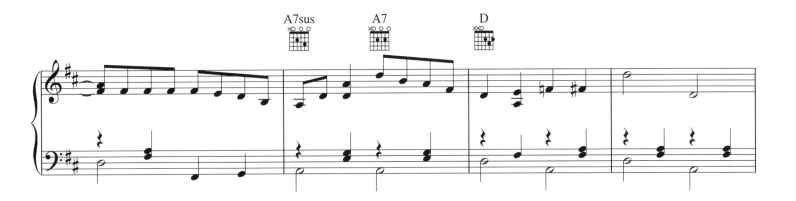

I'll _____ fly a - way, oh, glo - ry, ____

I'll _____ fly a - way in the morn - in'.

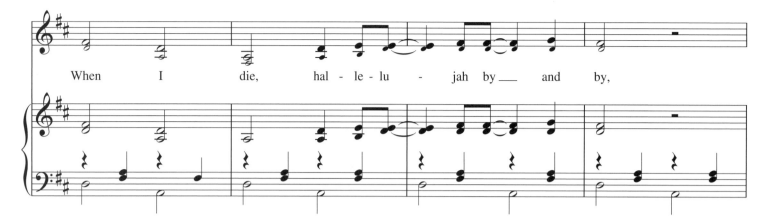

When I die, hal - le - lu - jah by ___ and by,

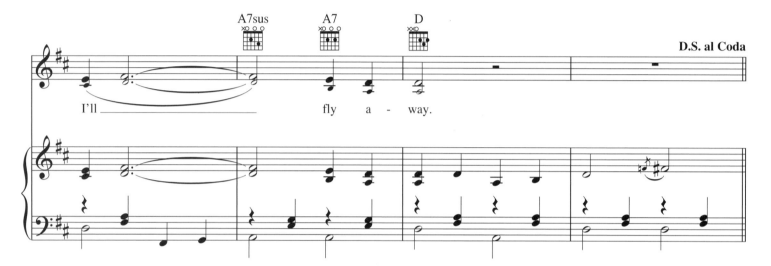

A7sus A7 D

D.S. al Coda

I'll _____ fly a - way.

CODA D

way. I'll _____

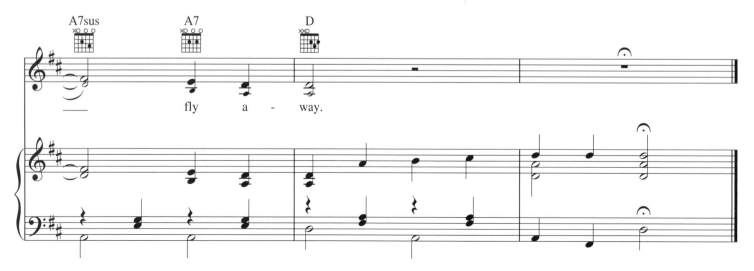

A7sus A7 D

___ fly a - way.

I'M BLUE, I'M LONESOME

Words and Music by BILL MONROE
and HANK WILLIAMS

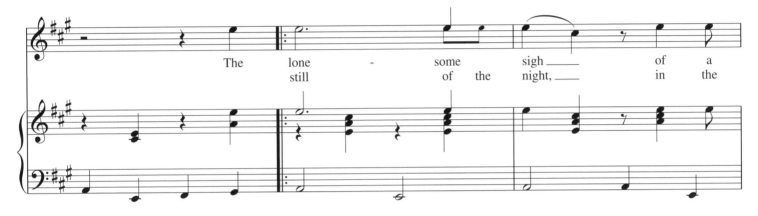

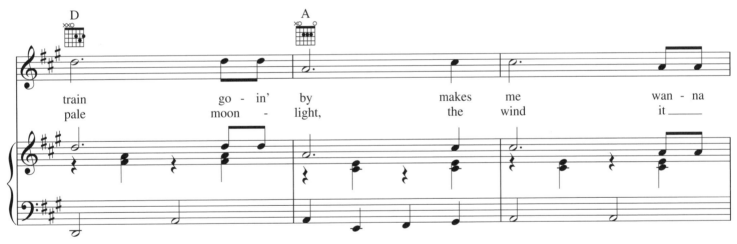

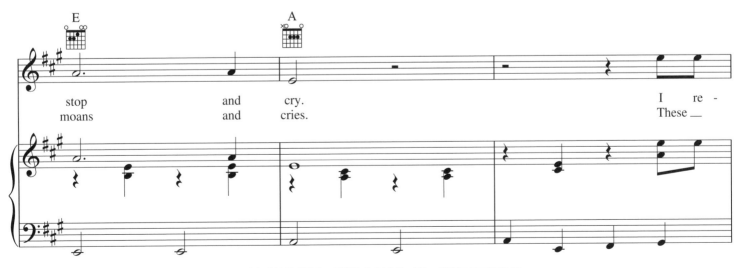

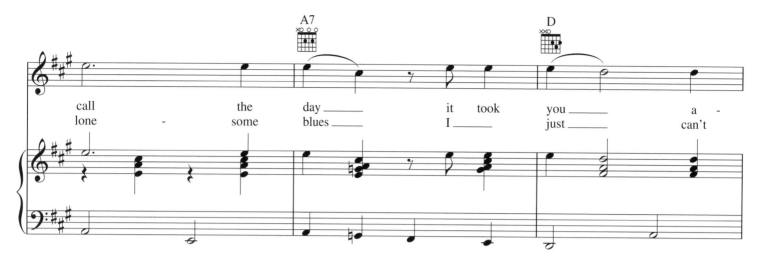

call
lone - some
the
day _____
it took
you _____
a -

lone -
some
blues _____
I _____
just _____
can't

way.
lose.
I'm
blue,
I'm
lone - some,

too.
When
I

hear _____
that
whis - tle
blow, _____

I wan - na pack my clothes _____ and

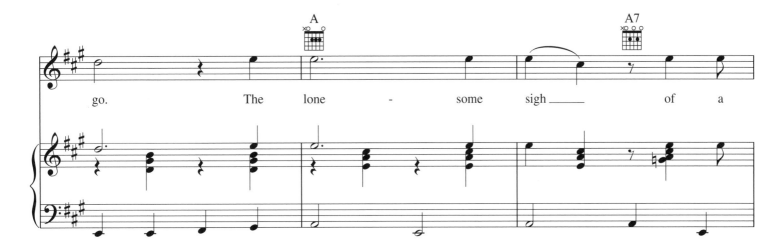

go. The lone - some sigh _____ of a

train go - in' by makes me wan - na

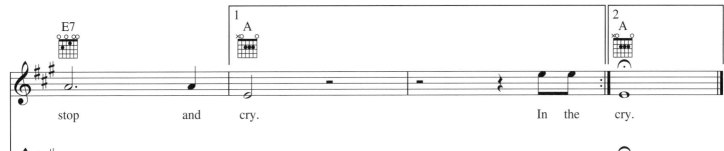

stop and cry. In the cry.

IF I LOSE

Words and Music by
RALPH STANLEY

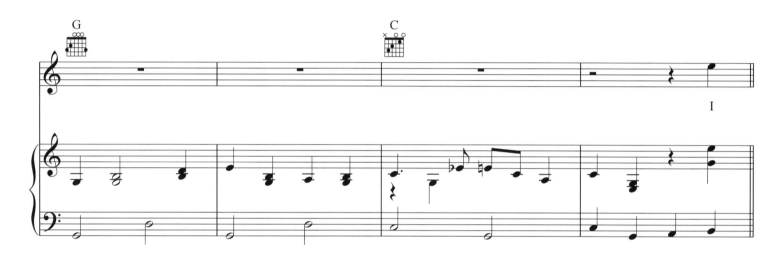

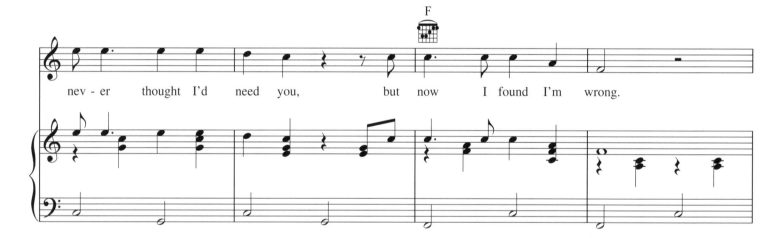

nev - er thought I'd need you, but now I found I'm wrong.

Come on back, sweet ma - ma, back where you be - long.

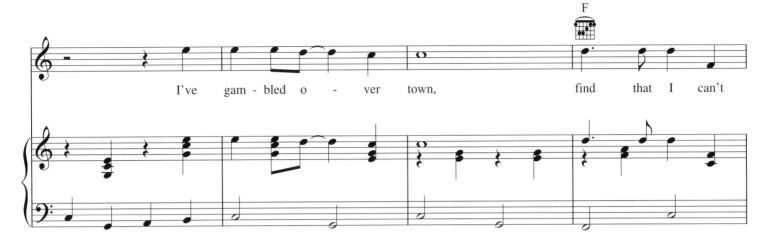

I've gam-bled o - ver town, find that I can't

win. Come on back and pick me up a - gain. ___

Now if I lose, let me lose. ___

I don't care _____ how much I lose.

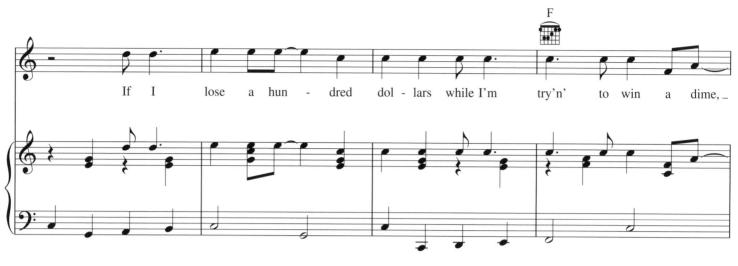

If I lose a hun - dred dol - lars while I'm try'n' to win a dime, __

__ my ba - by she's __ got mon - ey all the time. __

To Coda

Of all the oth - er gals I know, none can take your

place, 'cause when I get in - to a jam, they just ain't in the

race. So, now that you're back, dear, let's

take an - oth - er round. With you here by my side, dear, the

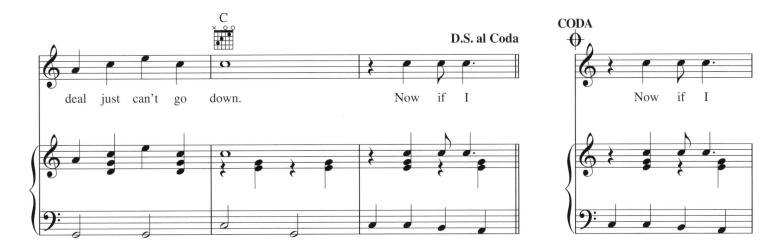

deal just can't go down. Now if I

Now if I

lose,   let me lose. ___   I don't

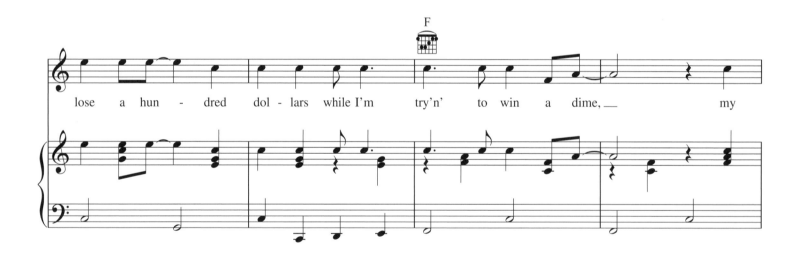

care _____ how much I lose.   If I

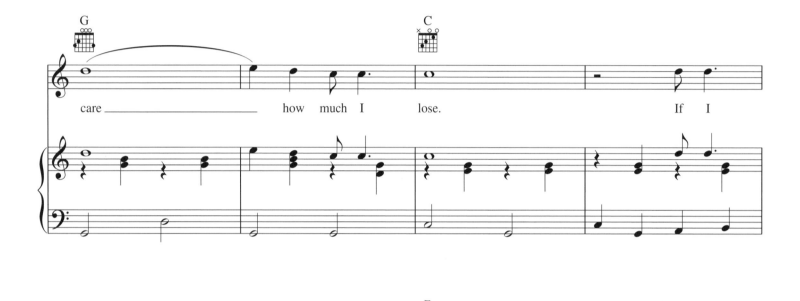

lose a hun - dred dol - lars while I'm try'n' to win a dime, __ my

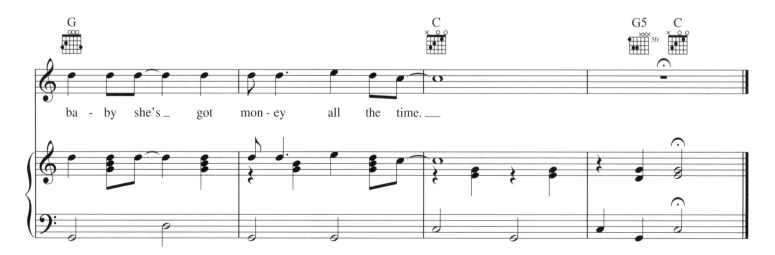

ba - by she's __ got mon - ey all the time. __

KNOCKIN' ON YOUR DOOR

Words and Music by VASSAR CLEMENTS,
JERRY GARCIA, DAVID GRISMAN,
JOHN KAHN and PETER ROWAN

Fast Bluegrass

I'm knock-in' on your door a-gain, my dar-lin'.
knock-in' on your door a-gain, my dar-lin',
bye, ___ dear, I know you'll soon for-get me.

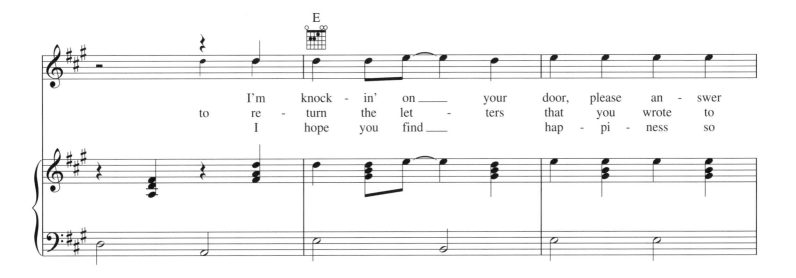

I'm knock-in' on ___ your door, please an-swer
to re-turn the let-ters that you wrote to
I hope you find ___ hap-pi-ness so

me.   I've tried to make you
me.   I nev-er read those
true.   When-ev-er you make

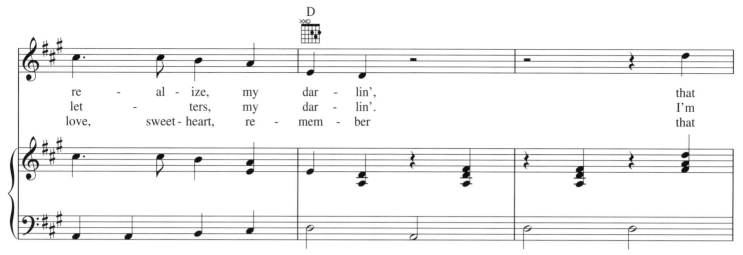

re - al - ize, my dar - lin', that
let - ters, my dar - lin'. I'm
love, sweet - heart, re - mem - ber that

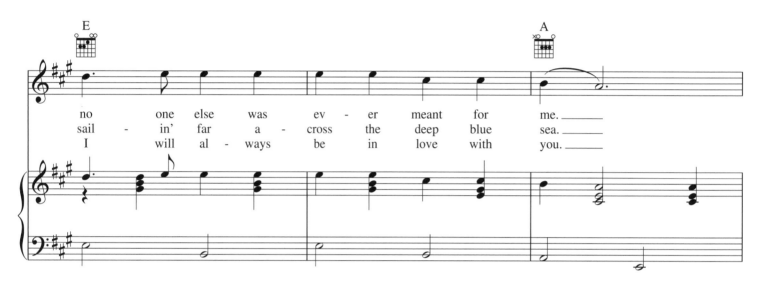

no one else was ev - er meant for me._____
sail - in' far a - cross the deep blue sea._____
I will al - ways be in love with you._____

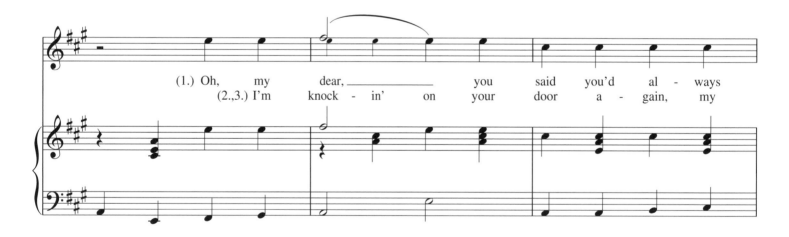

(1.) Oh, my dear,_____ you said you'd al - ways
(2.,3.) I'm knock - in' on your door a - gain, my

love me and prom - ised me your
dar - lin'. I'm knock - in' on your

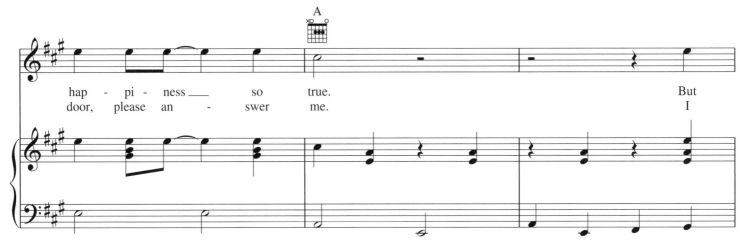

hap - pi - ness___ so true.
door, please an - swer me.

But
I

now you're gone a - way, dear, with an - oth - er.
nev - er read those let - ters,___ my dar - lin'.

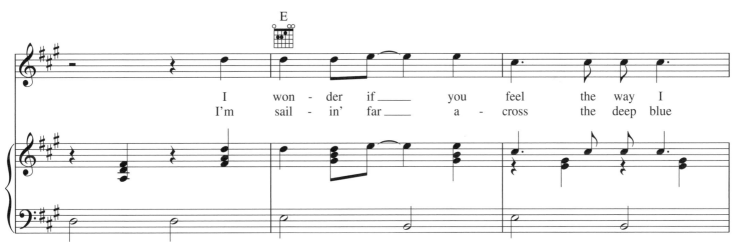

I won - der if___ you feel the way I
I'm sail - in' far___ a - cross the deep blue

do.___
sea.___

I'm sea.___
Good -

IN THE PINES

Traditional

six o' - clock, and cab passed by at nine.

Chorus

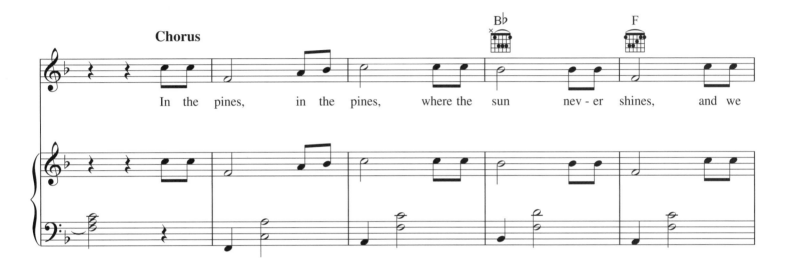

In the pines, in the pines, where the sun nev - er shines, and we

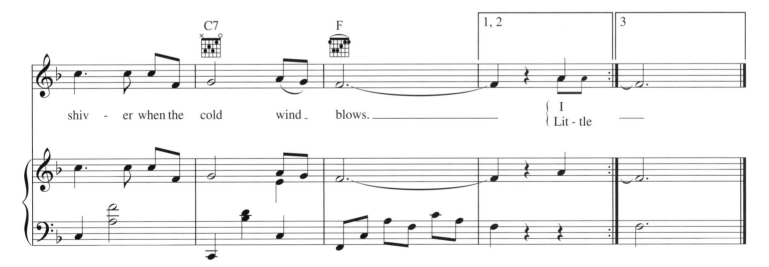

shiv - er when the cold wind _ blows. _____ I Lit - tle

Additional Lyrics

2. I asked my captain for the time of day,
   He said he threw his watch away.
   A long steel ram and a short cross tie,
   I'm on my way back home.
   Chorus

3. Little girl, little girl, what have I done,
   That makes you treat me so?
   You caused me to weep, you caused me to mourn,
   You cause me to leave my home.
   Chorus

KEEP ON THE SUNNY SIDE

Words and Music by
A.P. CARTER

Moderate Country

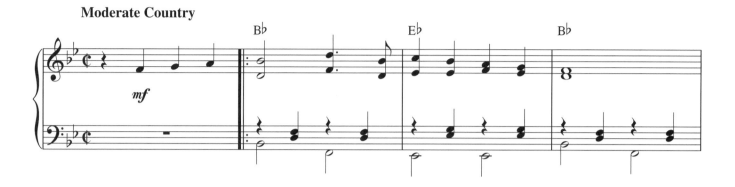

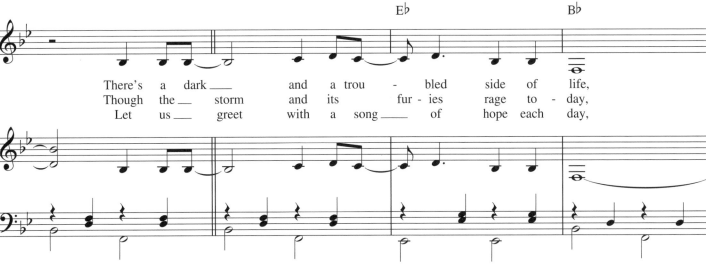

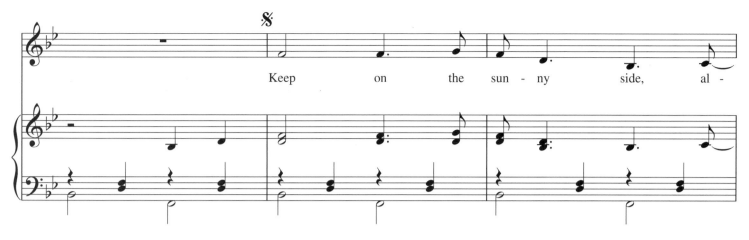

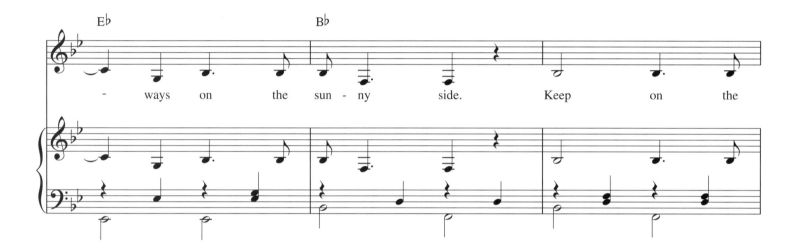

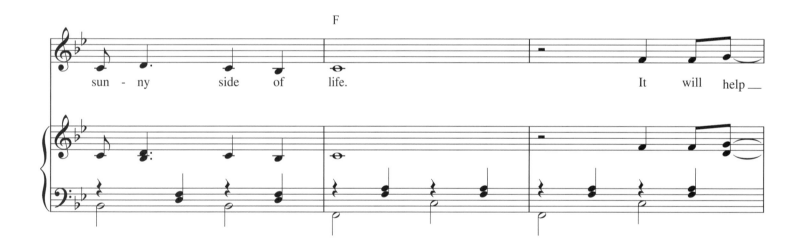

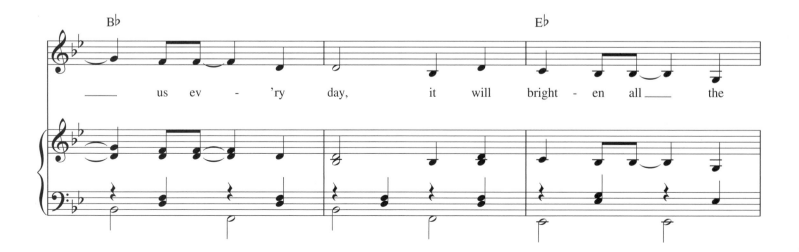

KENTUCKY WALTZ

Words and Music by
BILL MONROE

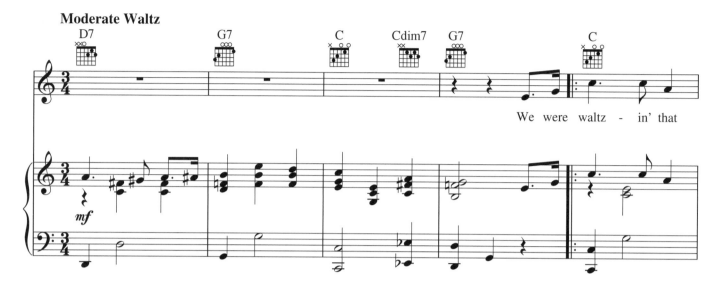

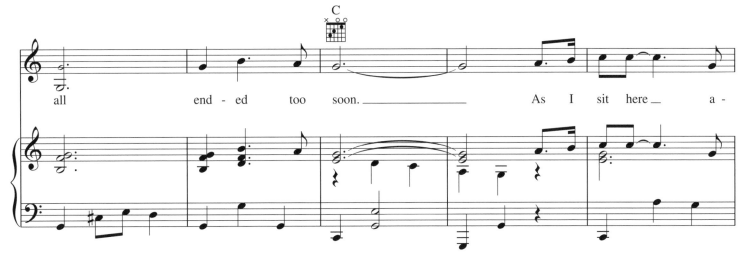

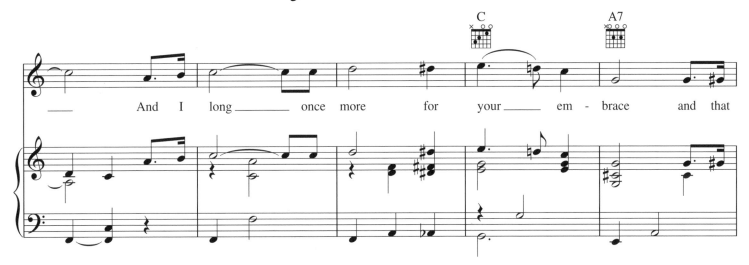

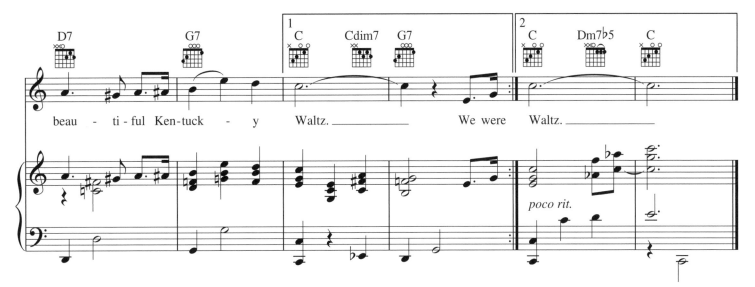

THE LONG BLACK VEIL

Words and Music by MARIJOHN WILKIN
and DANNY DILL

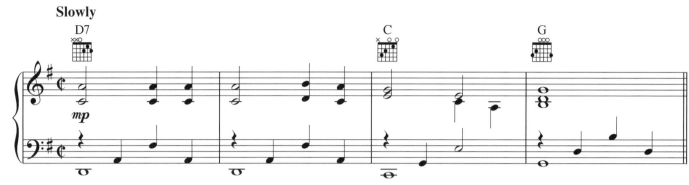

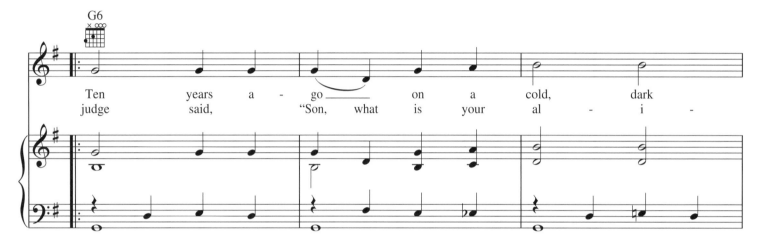

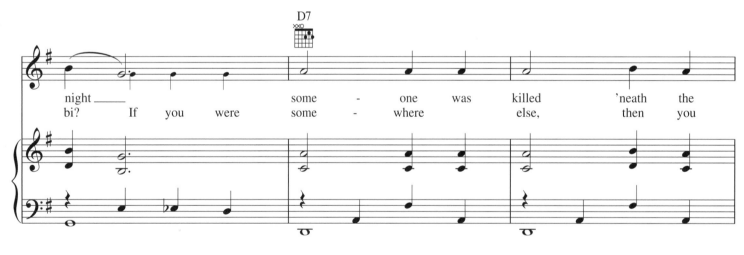

Ten years a - go _____ on a cold, dark
judge said, "Son, what is your al - i -

night _____ some - one was killed 'neath the
bi? If you were some - where else, then you

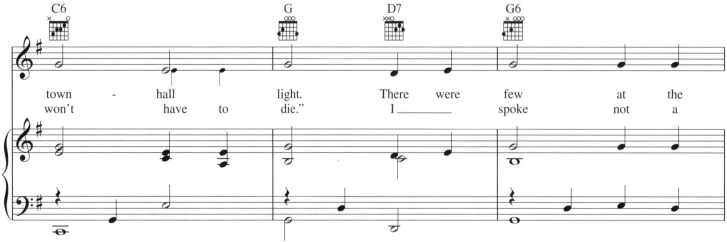

town - hall light. There were few at the
won't have to die." I _____ spoke not a

scene, ____ but they all a - greed ____ that the
word, al - though it all meant my life, for I had

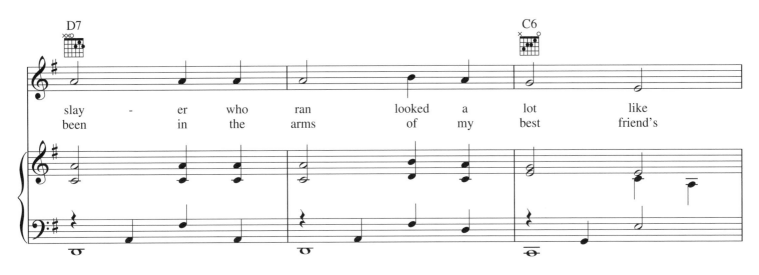

slay - er who ran looked a lot like
been - er in the arms of my best friend's

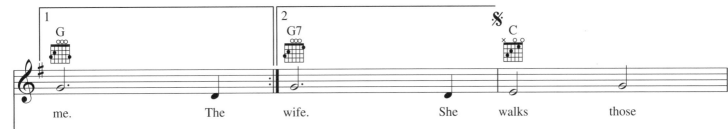

me. The wife. She walks those

hills in a long black veil; she vis - its my

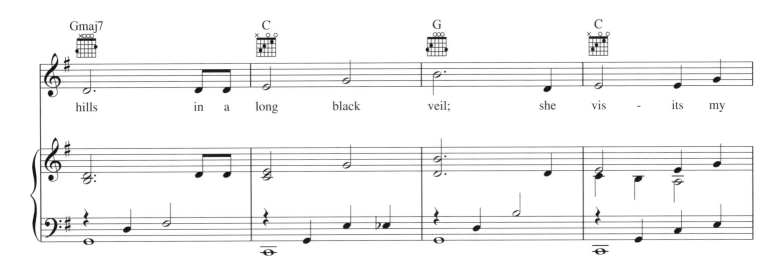

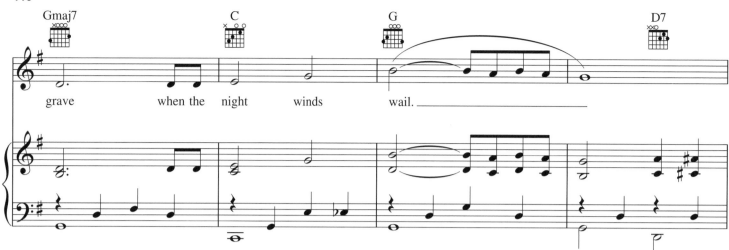

grave when the night winds wail.

No - bod - y knows, no - bod - y sees,

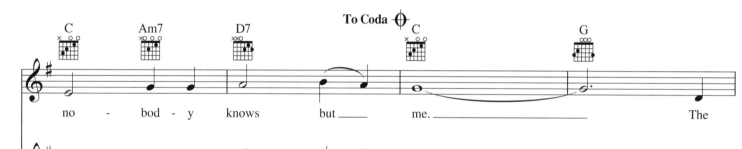

no - bod - y knows but me. The

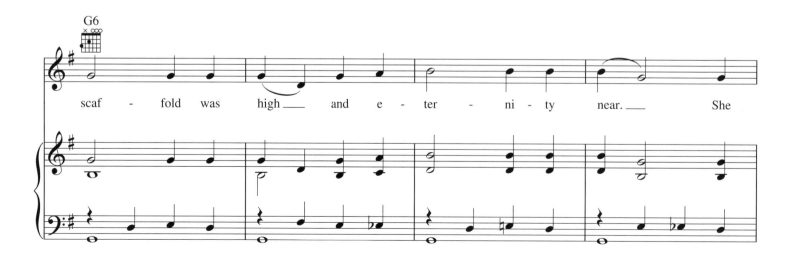

scaf - fold was high and e - ter - ni - ty near. She

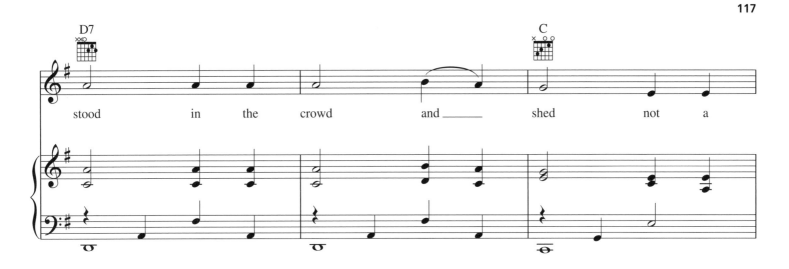

stood in the crowd and _____ shed not a

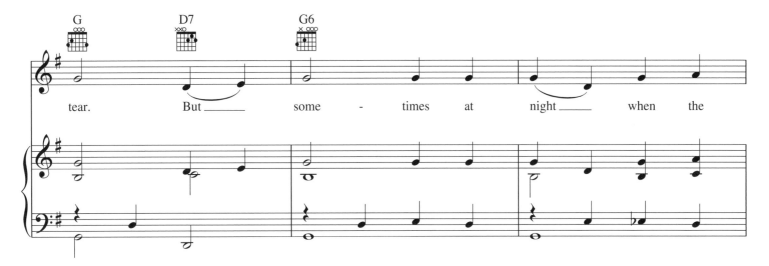

tear. But _____ some - times at night _____ when the

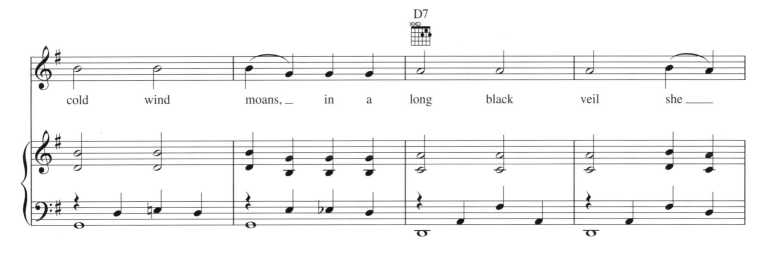

cold wind moans, _ in a long black veil she _____

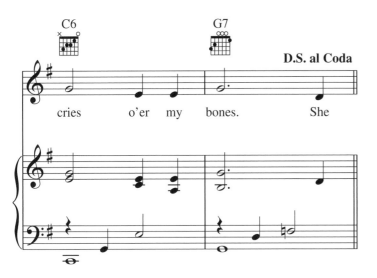

cries o'er my bones. She

D.S. al Coda

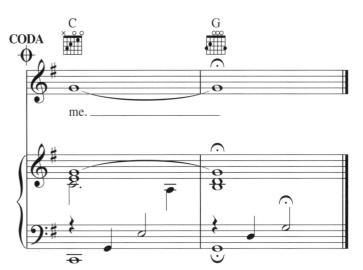

CODA

me. _____

MIDNIGHT MOONLIGHT

Words and Music by
PETER ROWAN

119

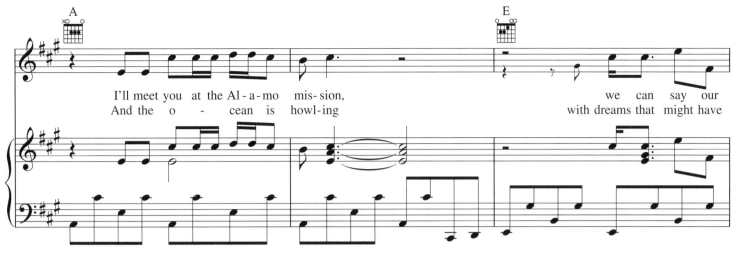

I'll meet you at the Al - a - mo mis- sion,   we can say our
And the o - cean is howl- ing   with dreams that might have

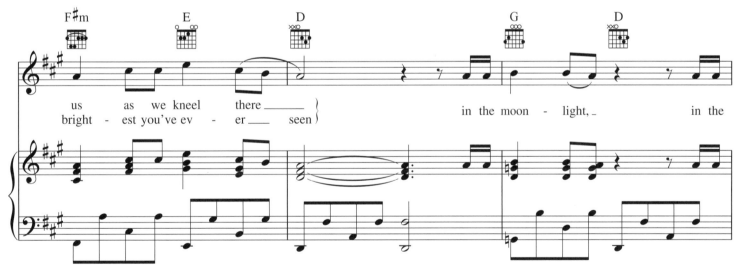

prayers.   The Ho - ly Ghost and the Vir - gin Moth-er will heal_____
been.   That last good morn-ing sun - rise will be the

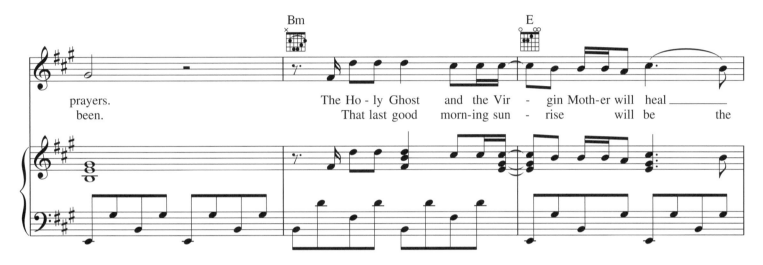

us as we kneel there_____ }   in the moon - light, _ in the
bright - est you've ev - er ___ seen }

mid - night, _ in the moon - light mid-night moon- light.   In the

moon - light, _ in the mid - night, _ in the moon - light mid-night moon-

light.

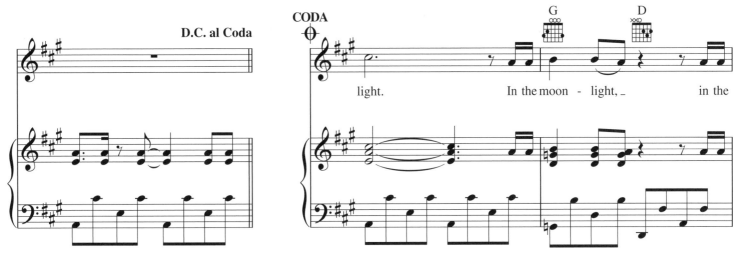

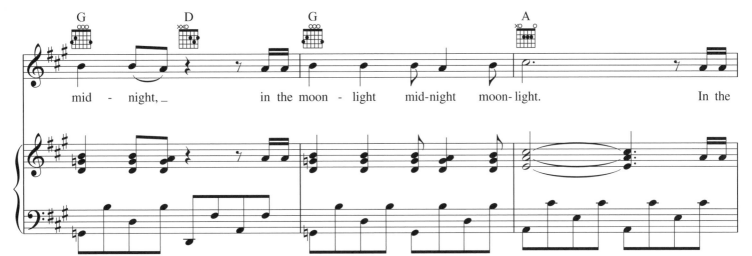

MOLLY AND TEN BROOKS

Words and Music by
BILL MONROE

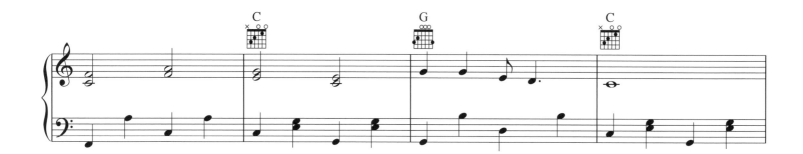

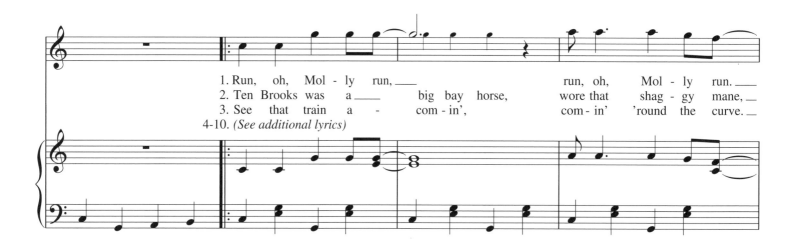

1. Run, oh, Mol - ly run, ___ run, oh, Mol - ly run. ___
2. Ten Brooks was a ___ big bay horse, wore that shag - gy mane, ___
3. See that train a - com - in', com - in' 'round the curve. ___
4-10. *(See additional lyrics)*

Ten Brooks gon - na beat you to the bright shin - in'
run all 'round ___ Mem - phis, he beat the Mem - phis
See old Ten Brooks run - nin', ___ he's strain - in' ev - 'ry

Additional Lyrics

4. Ten Brooks said to Molly what makes your head so red?
Runnin' in the hot sun puts fever in my head
Fever in my head O Lord, fever in my head.

5. Molly said to Ten Brooks you're lookin' mighty squirrel
Ten Brooks said to Molly I'm a-leavin' this old world
Leavin' this old world, O Lord, leavin' this old world.

6. Out in California where Molly done as she pleased
Come back to old Kentucky got beat with all ease
Beat with all ease, O Lord, beat with all ease.

7. The women all a-laughin' the child'n all a cryin'
The men all a-hollerin' old Ten Brooks a-flyin'
Old Ten Brooks a-flyin', O Lord, old Ten Brooks a-flyin'.

8. Kyper Kyper you're not a-ridin' right
Molly's beatin' old Ten Brooks clear out sight
Clear out of sight, O Lord, clear out of sight.

9. Kyper Kyper Kyper my son
Give old Ten Brooks the bridle let old Ten Brooks run
Let old Ten Brooks run, O Lord, let old Ten Brooks run.

10. Go and catch old Ten Brooks and hitch him in the shade
We're gonna bury old Molly in a coffin ready made
Coffin ready made, O Lord, coffin ready made.

MORE PRETTY GIRLS THAN ONE

American Folk Song

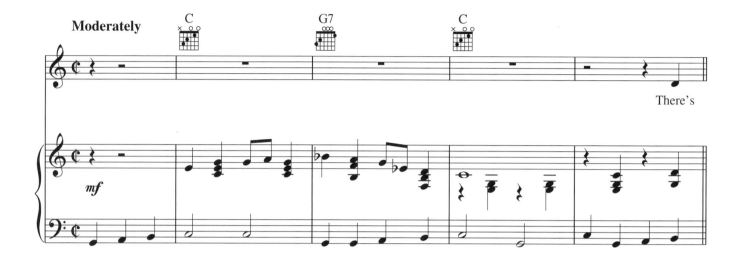

There's

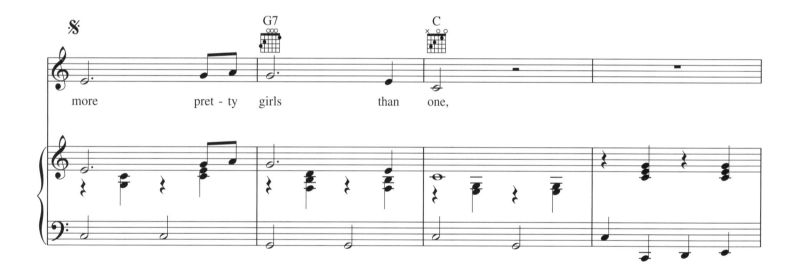

more   pret - ty   girls   than   one,

more   pret - ty   girls   than   one.

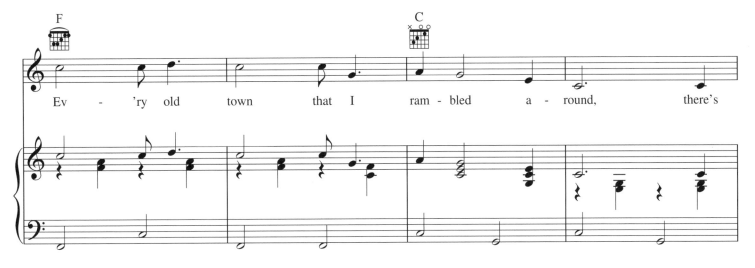

Ev - 'ry old town that I ram - bled a - round, there's

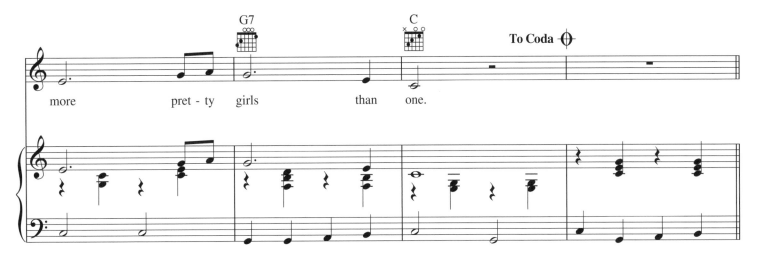

more pret - ty girls than one.

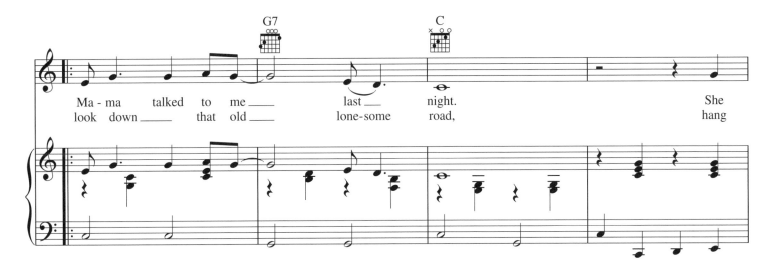

Ma - ma talked to me ___ last ___ night. She
look down ___ that old ___ lone-some road, hang

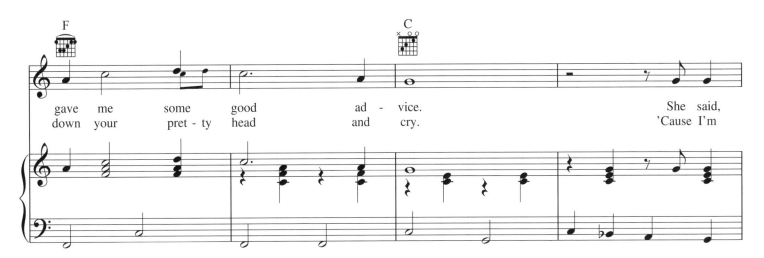

gave me some good ad - vice. She said,
down your pret - ty head and cry. 'Cause I'm

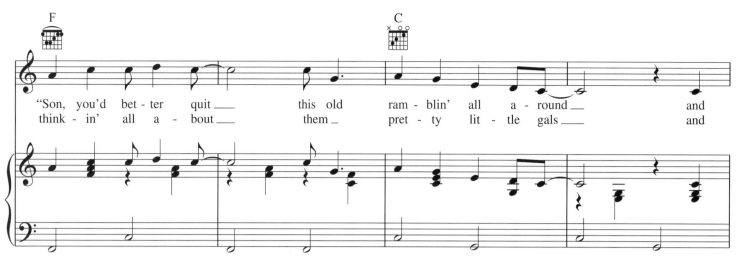

F ... **C**

"Son, you'd bet - ter quit ___ this old ram - blin' all a - round ___ and
think - in' all a - bout ___ them ___ pret - ty lit - tle gals ___ and

G7 ... **C**

1

mar - ry you a sweet ___ lit - tle wife." Hon - ey,
hop - in' that I nev - er ___ die.

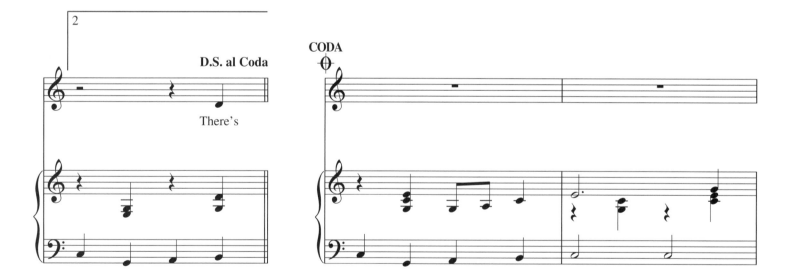

2

D.S. al Coda

There's

CODA

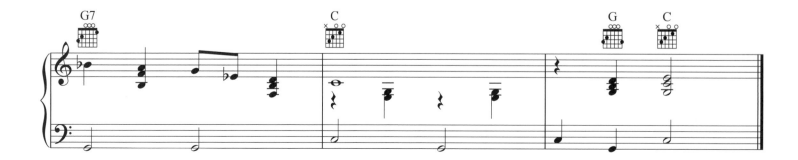

G7 ... **C** ... **G** **C**

NELLIE KANE

Words and Music by
TIM O'BRIEN

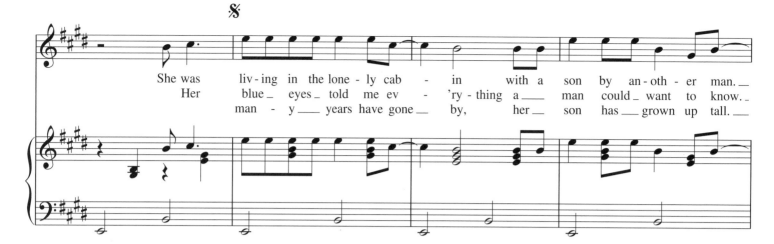

She was liv-ing in the lone-ly cab - in with a son by an-oth-er man.
Her blue eyes told me ev - 'ry-thing a man could want to know.
man - y years have gone by, her son has grown up tall.

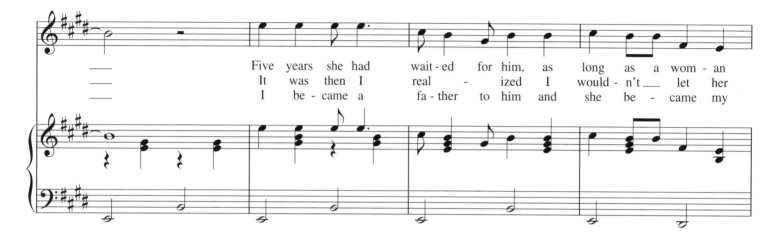

Five years she had wait-ed for him, as long as a wom - an
It was then I real - ized I would-n't let her
I be-came a fa - ther to him and she be - came my

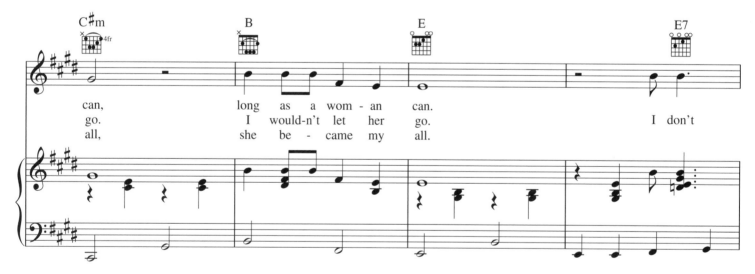

C#m   B   E   E7

can,   long as a wom - an can.
go.   I would-n't let her go.   I don't
all,   she be - came my all.

A   E

know   what changed my mind.   Till then I

was _____ the ram-blin' kind. The kind of

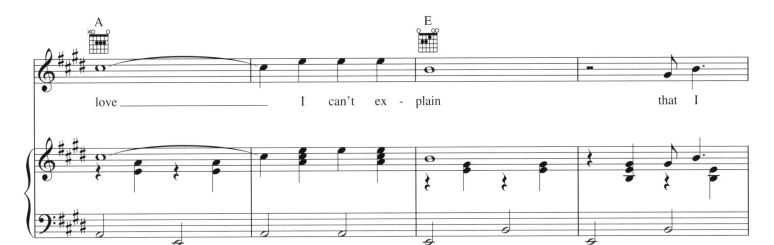

love _____ I can't ex-plain that I

have _____ for Nel-lie Kane. ___

She

Now

D.S. al Coda

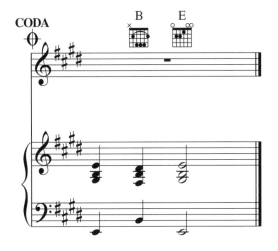

CODA

OLD HOME PLACE

Words by MITCHELL F. JAYNE
Music by RODNEY DILLARD

long to be, a place that I call home.					A

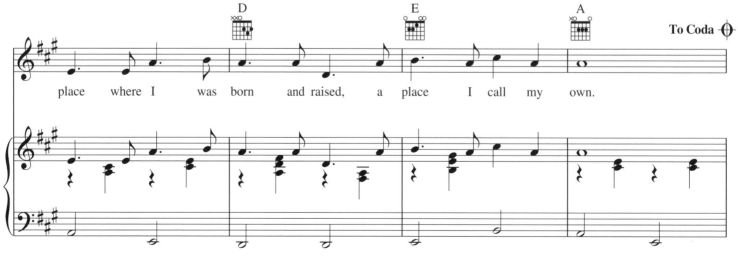

place where I was born and raised, a place I call my own.

To Coda

Ev -'ry night up - on my porch, I'd hear the whip-poor-
A bare-foot boy that roamed the hills, so com - mon and so

will,
plain,

sing-in' to me that lone - some sound,
tells _ his life just how it was, the

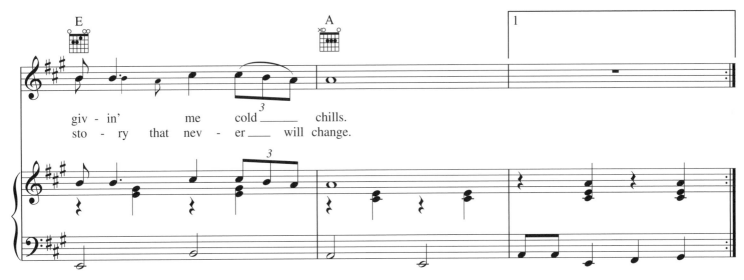

giv - in' me cold _ chills.
sto - ry that nev - er _ will change.

D.S. al Coda

CODA

A place I call my _ own.

ONCE MORE

Words and Music by
ROBERT OWENS

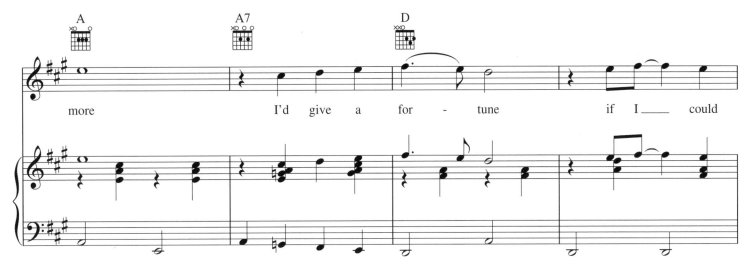

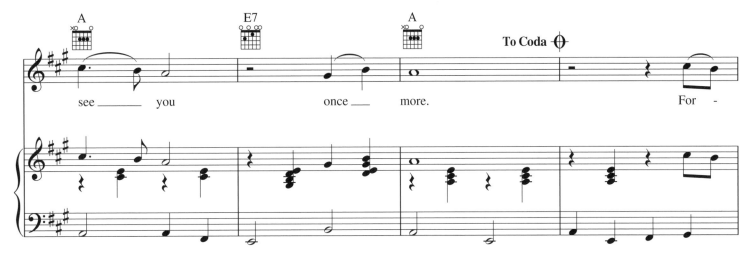

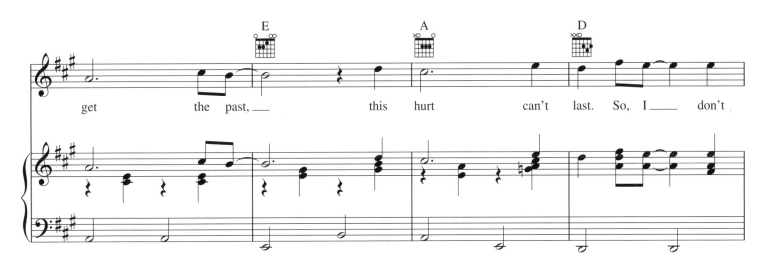

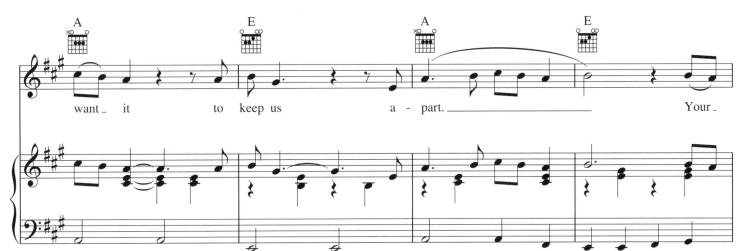

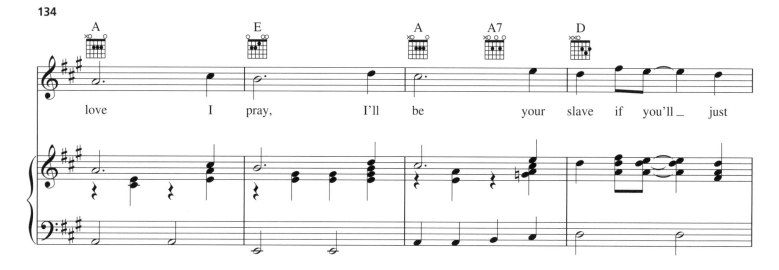

love   I pray,   I'll be   your slave if you'll __ just

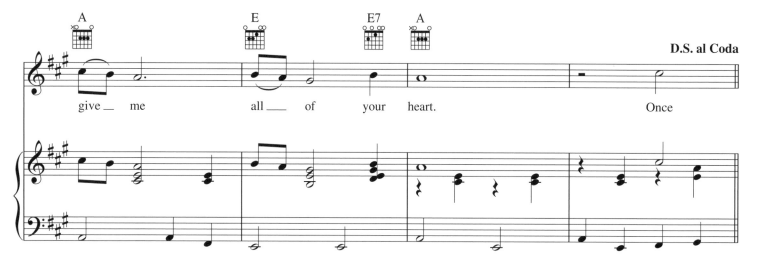

D.S. al Coda

give __ me   all ___ of   your   heart.   Once

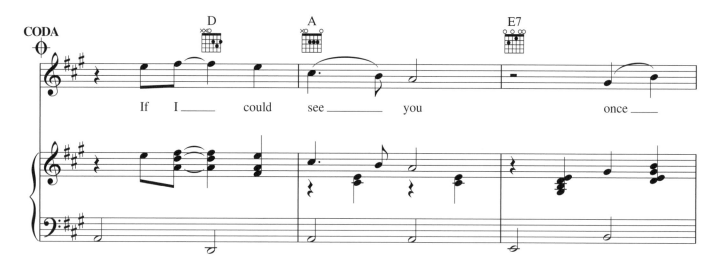

CODA

If I ___   could   see _____ you   once ____

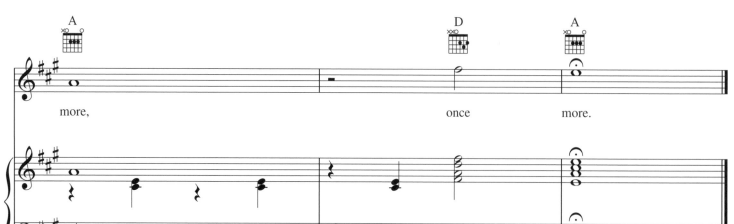

more,   once   more.

PANAMA RED

Words and Music by
PETER ROWAN

Pan-a-ma Red, Pan-a-ma Red,

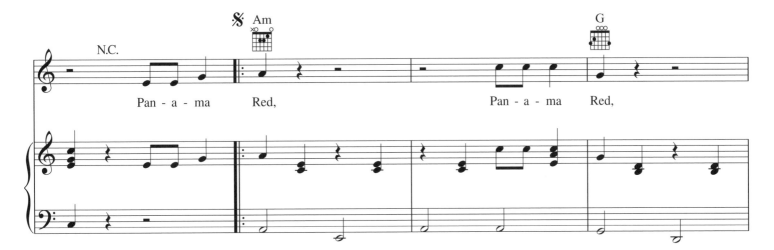

he'll steal your wom-an, then he'll rob your head.

Pan-a-ma Red, Pan-a-ma Red,

on his white horse Mes-ca-li-to___ he come breez-in' through town.___

___ Bet your wom-an is up in bed___ with old Pan-a-ma

To Coda ⊕

Red.

{ The judge don't know when Red's in town. He keeps well
{ Ev-'ry-bod-y's look-in' out for him 'cause

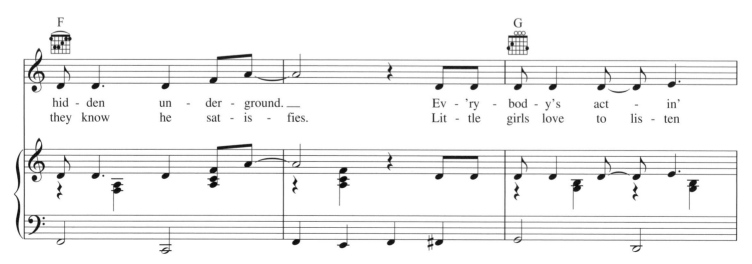

hid-den un-der-ground.___ Ev-'ry-bod-y's act - in'
they know he sat-is-fies. Lit-tle girls love to lis-ten

la - zy, fall - in' out ___ and hang - in' 'round. My wom - an said, ___ "Hey,
to him sing ___ and tell sweet lies. When things get too ___ con -

Pe - dro, you're act - in' cra - zy like a clown." ___ No - bod - y feels ___ like
fus - in', hon - ey, we're bet - ter off in bed. ___ I'll be search - in' all ___ the

work - in', Pan - a - ma Red is back in town. Pan - a - ma
joints in town ___ for Pan - a - ma

Red. Pan - a - ma

D.S. al Coda

CODA

Red.

ROCKY TOP

Words and Music by BOUDLEAUX BRYANT
and FELICE BRYANT

Wish that I was on ol' Rock-y Top,
Once two stran-gers climbed ol' Rock-y Top,

down in the Ten-nes-see hills.
look-in' for a moon-shine still.

Ain't no smog-gy smoke on Rock-y Top, ain't no tel-e-phone
Stran-gers ain't come down from Rock-y Top; reck-on they nev-er

bills.
will.
Once I had a girl on Rock-y Top;
Corn won't grow at all on Rock-y Top;
I've had years of cramped-up cit-y life,

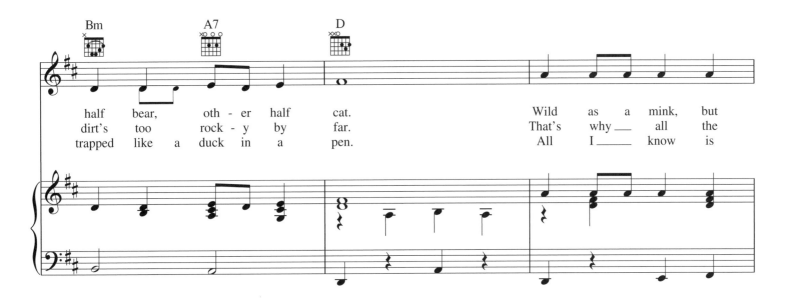

half bear, oth-er half cat.
dirt's too rock-y by far.
trapped like a duck in a pen.
Wild as a mink, but
That's why all the
All I know is

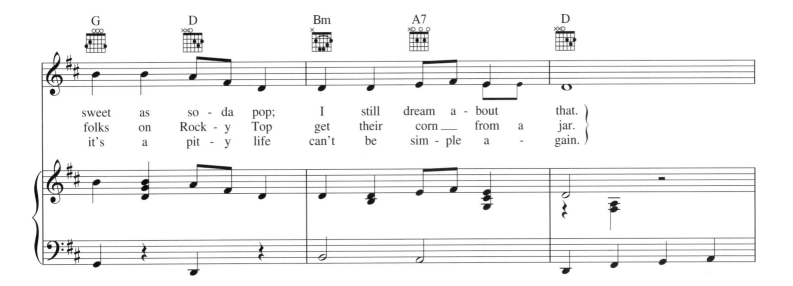

sweet as so-da pop; I still dream a-bout that.
folks on Rock-y Top get their corn from a jar.
it's a pit-y life can't be sim-ple a-gain.

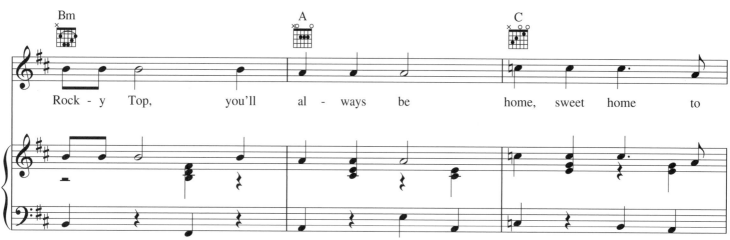

SALTY DOG BLUES

Words and Music by WILEY A. MORRIS
and ZEKE MORRIS

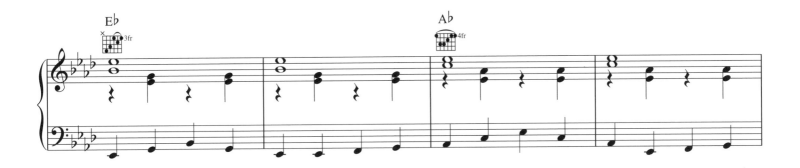

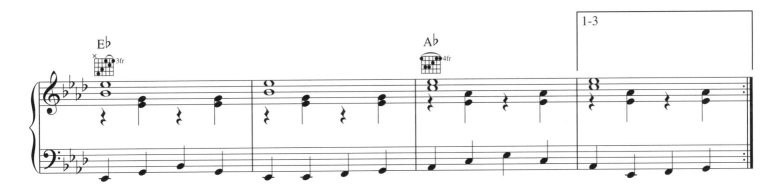

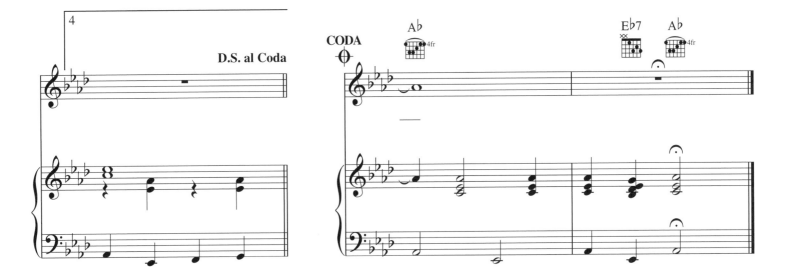

SITTING ON TOP OF THE WORLD

Words and Music by WALTER JACOBS
and LONNIE CARTER

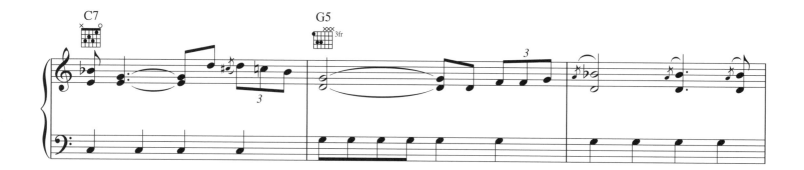

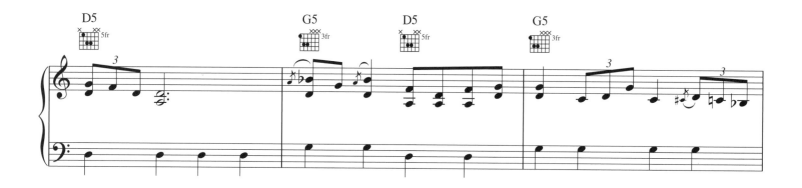

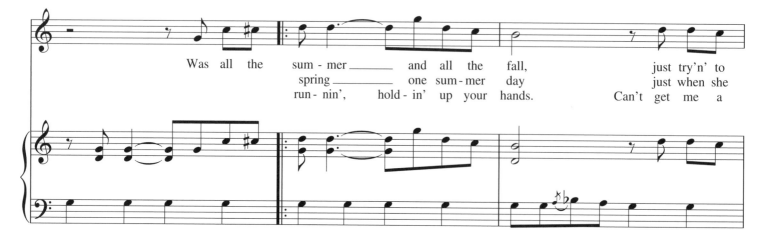

Was all the sum-mer _____ and all the fall, just try'n' to
spring _____ one sum-mer day just when she
run-nin', hold-in' up your hands. Can't get me a

find my   lit - tle   Le —   nore.   But now she's gone ⎞
left me,   she's gone to   stay.   But now she's gone ⎬   and I ___ don't
wom-an   quick as you can get a   man.   But now you're gone ⎠

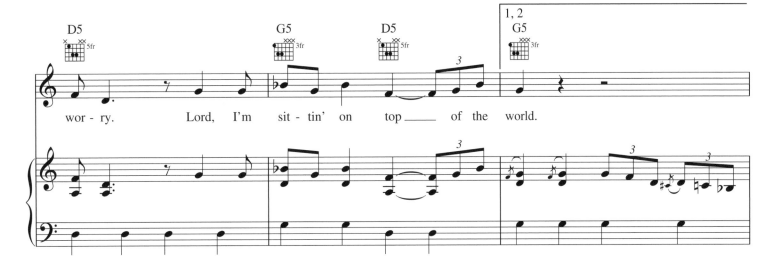

wor - ry.   Lord, I'm sit - tin' on   top _____ of the world.

{ Was in the   world.
{ And you come

Half the days   I did-n't know your
sta-tion   down in the
days   they have gone

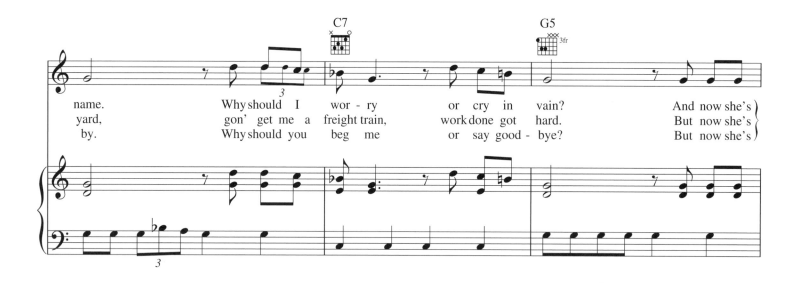

name.   Why should I   wor - ry   or cry in vain?   And now she's
yard,   gon' get me a   freight train,   work done got hard.   But now she's
by.   Why should you   beg me   or say good - bye?   But now she's

gone   and I don't wor - ry.   Lord, I'm sit - tin' on top _____ of the

world.

Went to the world.
Those lone-some

SOPHRONIE

Words and Music by ALTON DELMORE
and D.C. MULLINS

Moderately fast

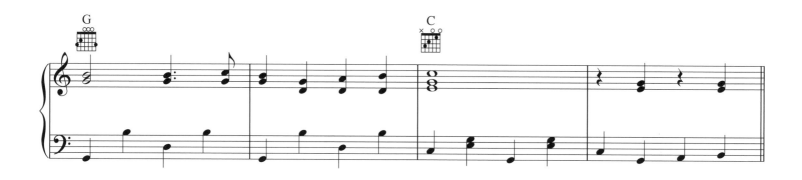

Love 'em and leave 'em, kiss 'em and grieve 'em, that used to

be my mot - to so high till my Soph - ro - nie

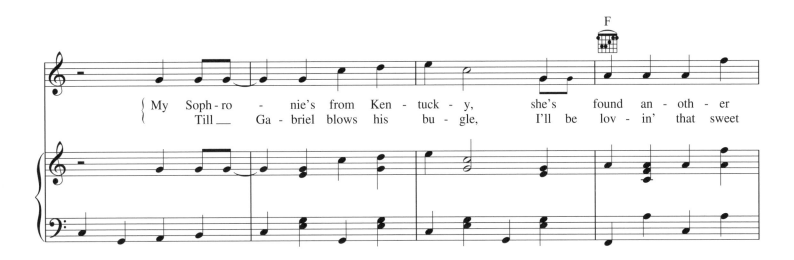

150

still up in the sky, now I'm just a hot shot with a
wom-en, me oh my,

tear-drop in my eye.

D.S. al Coda

1

2

CODA

WABASH CANNONBALL

Words and Music by
A.P. CARTER

Moderately

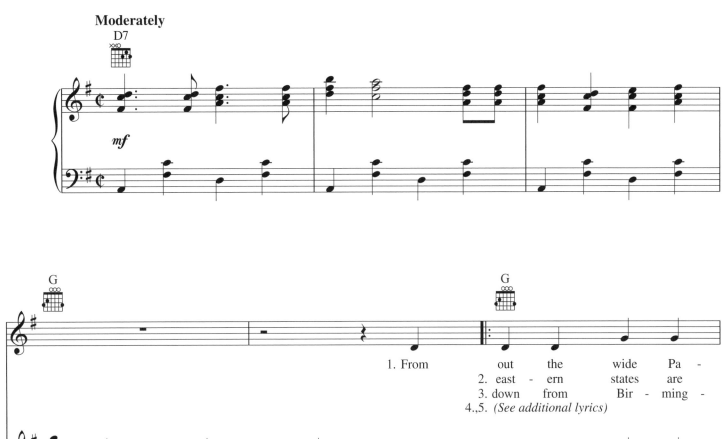

1. From out the wide Pa-
2. east - ern states are
3. down from Bir - ming -
4.,5. *(See additional lyrics)*

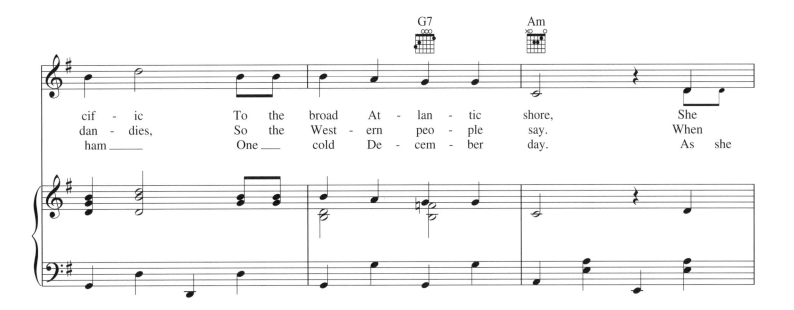

cif - ic   To the broad At - lan - tic shore,   She
dan - dies,   So the West - ern peo - ple say.   When
ham _____   One _____ cold De - cem - ber day.   As she

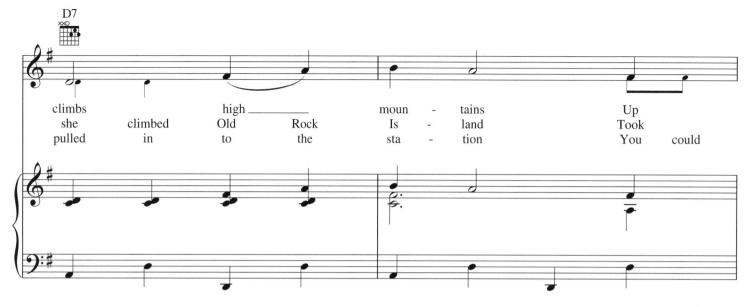

climbs   high _____   moun - tains   Up
she   climbed   Old   Rock   Is - land   Took
pulled   in   to   the   sta - tion   You   could

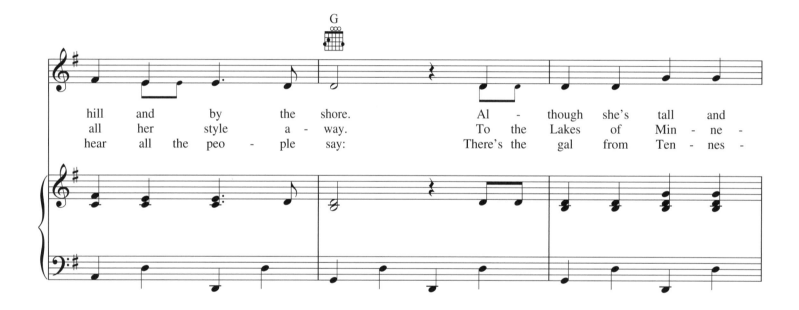

hill   and   by   the   shore.   Al - though she's tall and
all   her   style   a - way.   To   the   Lakes   of   Min - ne -
hear   all   the   peo - ple   say: There's   the   gal   from   Ten - nes -

hand - some   And she's known quite well by   all,   She's a
so - ta   Where the rip - pling wa - ters   fall,   No _____
see, _____   She   is   long   and   she   is   tall.   She _____

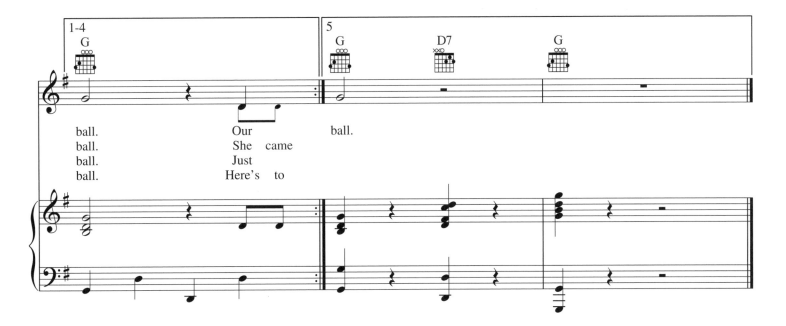

reg - 'lar com - bi - na - tion of the Wa - bash Can - non -
chang - es can be tak - en on the Wa - bash Can - non -
comes from Bir - ming - ham on the Wa - bash Can - non -

ball. Our ball.
ball. She came
ball. Just
ball. Here's to

Additional Lyrics

4. Just listen to the jingle
   And the rumble and the roar,
   As she glides along the woodland
   To the hills and by the shore.
   Hear the mighty rush of the engine
   Hear the lonesome hoboes call,
   While she's trav'ling thru the jungle
   On the Wabash Cannonball.

5. Here's to old man Daddy Claxton
   May his name forever stand;
   May it always be remembered
   Throughout the land.
   His earthly race is over
   And the curtains 'round him fall.
   We'll carry him home to vict'ry
   On the Wabash Cannonball.

TURN YOUR RADIO ON

Words and Music by
ALBERT E. BRUMLEY

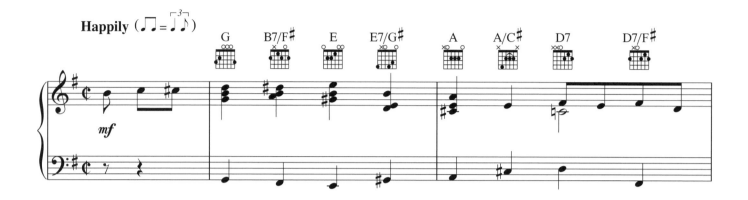

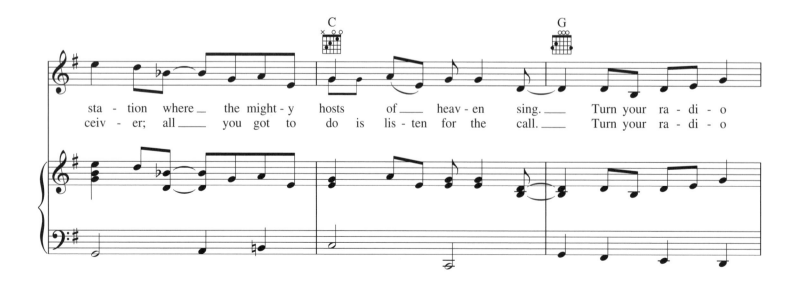

sta - tion where __ the might - y hosts of __ heav - en sing. __ Turn your ra - di - o
ceiv - er; all __ you got to do is lis - ten for the call. __ Turn your ra - di - o

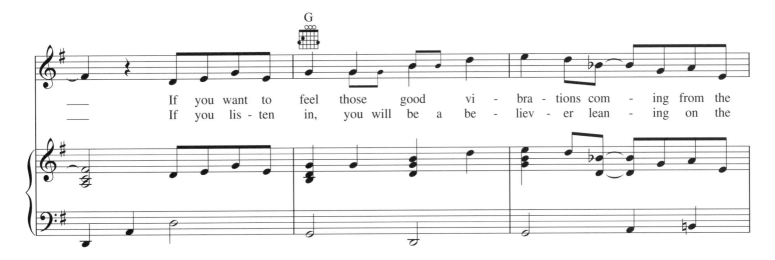

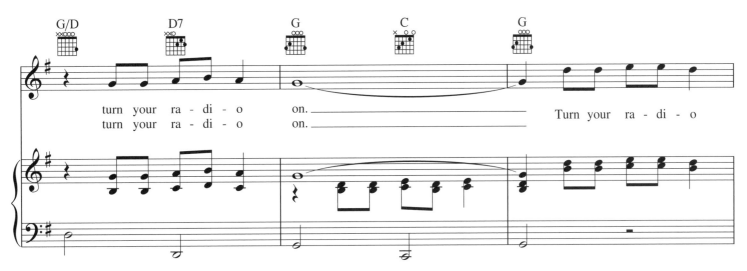

on _____ and lis-ten to the mu-sic in the air.__

__ Turn your ra-di-o on, ____ heav-en's glo-ry share.

__ Turn your lights down low ____

__ and lis-ten to the Mas-ter's ra-di-o.__ Get in touch with

God; _____ turn your ra - di - o on. _____

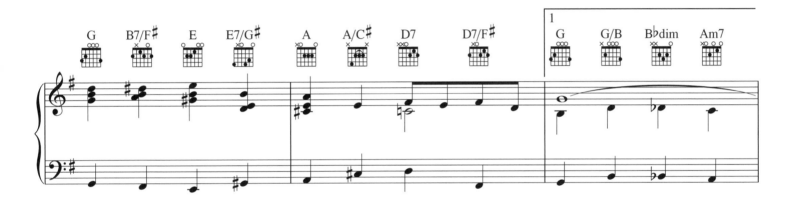

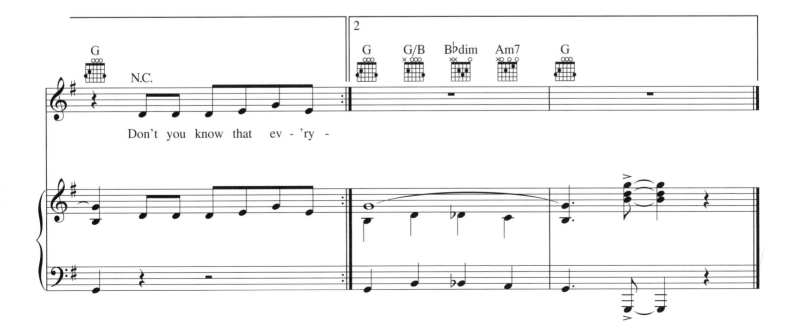

Don't you know that ev - 'ry -

WHAT WOULD YOU GIVE IN EXCHANGE FOR YOUR SOUL

Words and Music by J.H. CARR
and J.J. BERRY

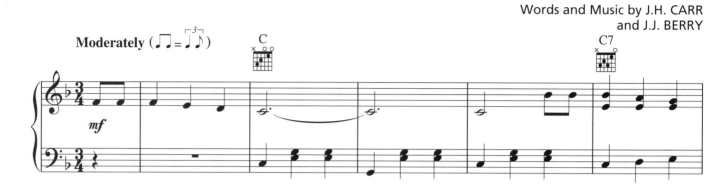

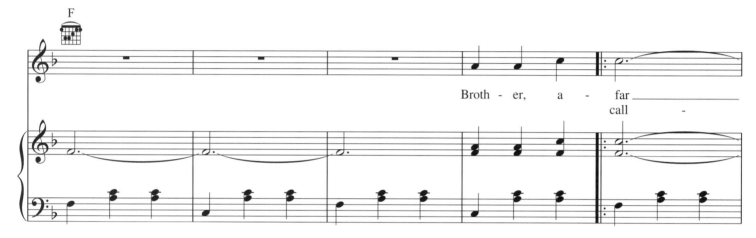

Broth - er, a - far _____ call -

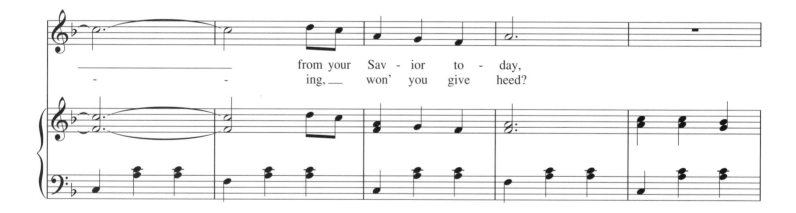

_____ from your Sav - ior to - day,
ing, ___ won' you give heed?

risk - ing your soul _____ for the
Must the dear Sav - ior ___

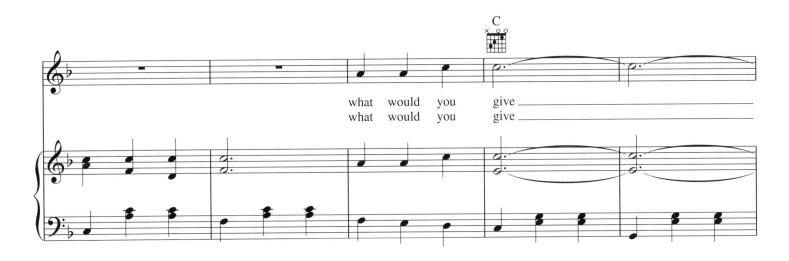

What would you give (in ex - change) what would you

give (in ex - change) what would you give _____

C

_____ in ex - change for your soul?

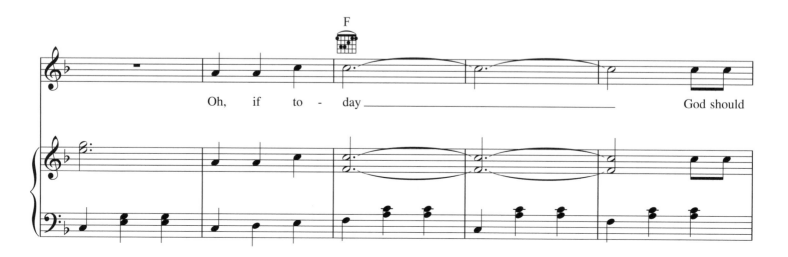

F

Oh, if to - day _____ God should

call you a - way,

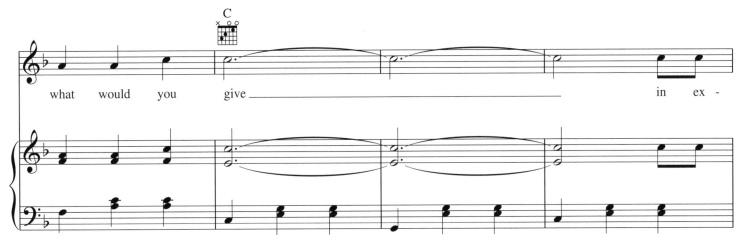

C

what would you give _____ in ex -

1

F

change for your soul?

2

F

Mer - cy is soul?

rit.

WITH BODY AND SOUL

Words and Music by
VIRGINIA STAUFFER

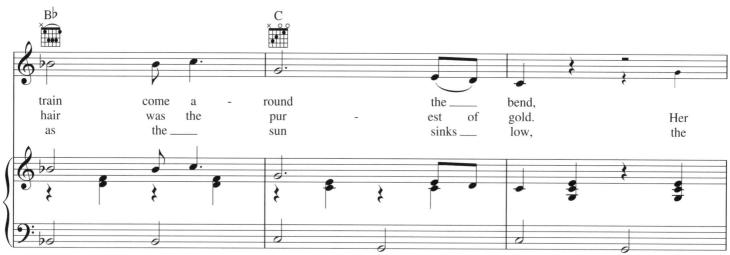

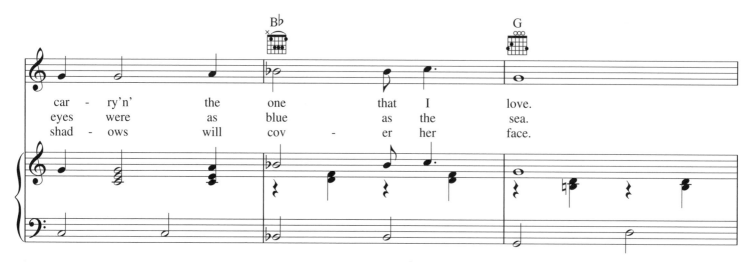

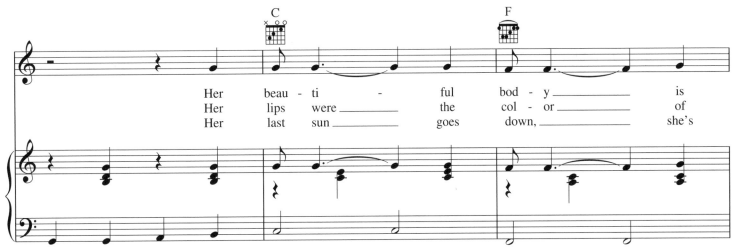

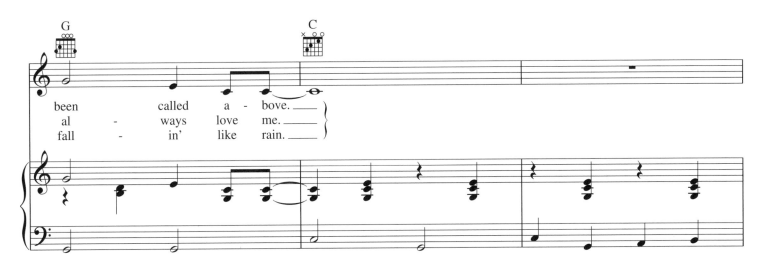

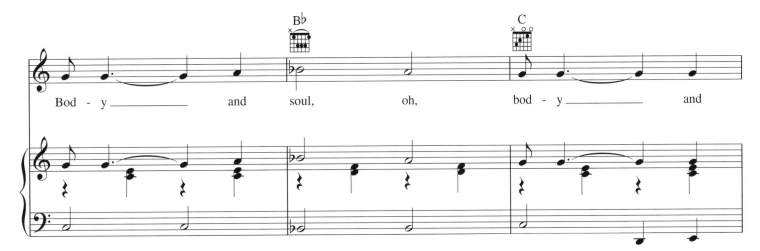

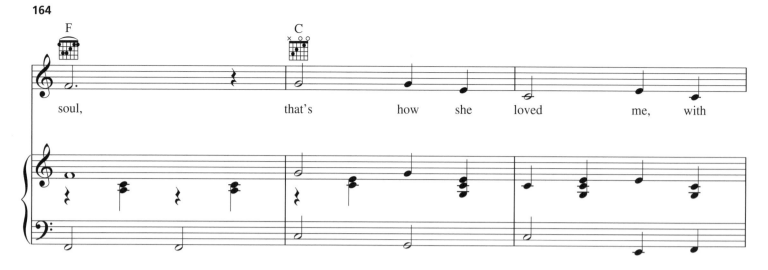

soul,   that's   how   she   loved   me,   with

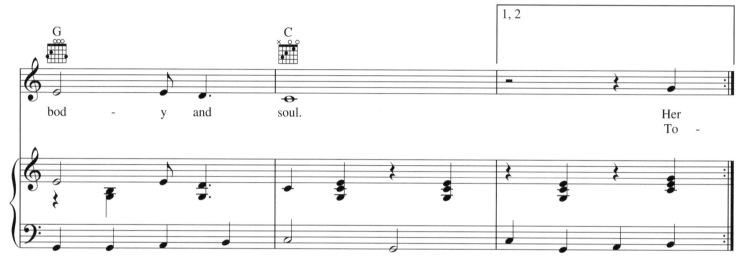

bod - y   and   soul.   Her

To -

That's   how   she   loved   me,   with

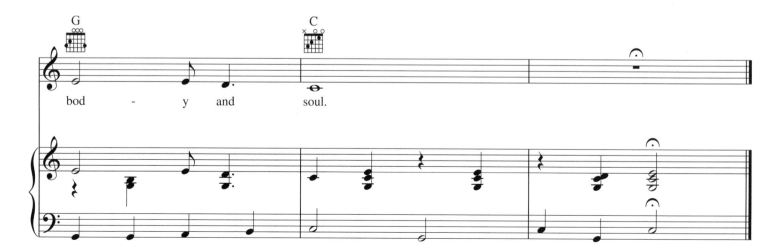

bod - y   and   soul.

THE WRECK OF THE OLD '97

Words and Music by HENRY WHITTER,
CHARLES NOELL and FRED LEWEY

Additional Lyrics

2. He turned and he said to his black greasy fireman,
"Just shovel on a little more coal,
And when we cross the White Oak Mountain
You can watch old 'ninety-seven' roll."

3. It's a mighty rough road from Lynchburg to Danville,
On a line on a three-mile grade.
It was on this grade that he lost his average,
You can see what a jump he made.

4. He was going down the grade makin' ninety miles an hour,
When his whistle broke into a scream.
They found him in the wreck with his hand on the throttle,
He was scalded to death by the steam.

5. Now, ladies, you must take warning,
From this time now on learn,
Never speak harsh words to your true loving husband,
He may leave you and never return.

Y'ALL COME

Words and Music by
ARLIE DUFF

When you live in the coun - try, ev - 'ry -
Kin - folks a - com - in', _____ they're
Grand - ma's a - wish - in' _____ they'd

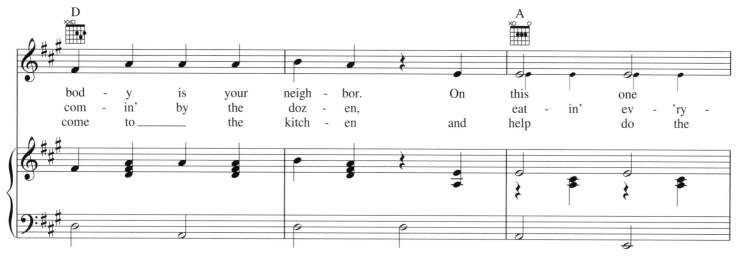

bod - y is your neigh - bor. On this one
com - in' by the doz - en, eat - in' ev - 'ry -
come to _____ the kitch - en and help do the

thing you can re - ly.
thing from soup to hay.
dish - es right a - way.

They'll
And
But

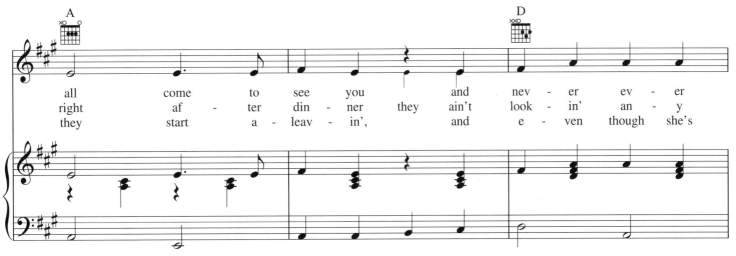

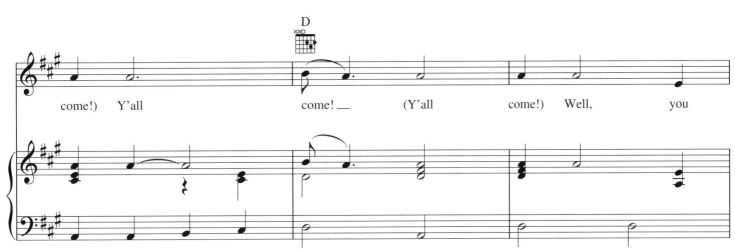

all come to see us now and then.

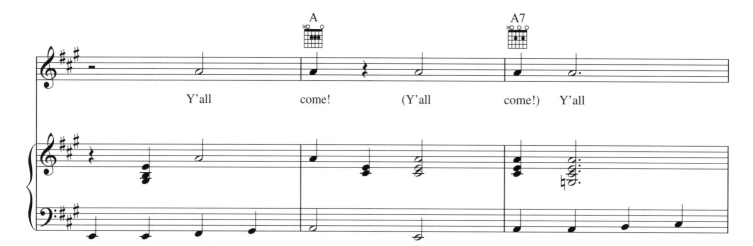

Y'all come! (Y'all come!) Y'all

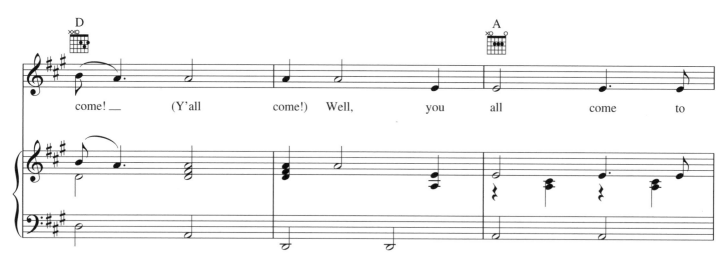

come! __ (Y'all come!) Well, you all come to

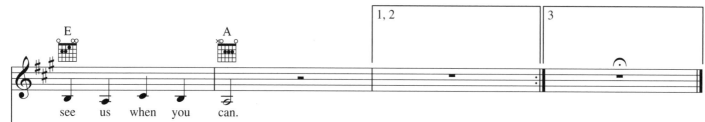

see us when you can.